Watch Me Grow

Watch Me Grow

Fun Ways to Learn About
Cells, Bones, Muscles, and Joints

Activities for Children 5 to 9

MICHELLE O'BRIEN-PALMER

CHICAGO REVIEW PRESS

Library of Congress Cataloging-in-Publication Data

O'Brien-Palmer, Michelle.
    Watch me grow : fun ways to learn about cells, bones, muscles,
    and joints : activities for children 5—9 / Michelle O'Brien-Palmer.
            p.   cm.
    Includes bibliographical references (p. 137).
    Summary: Explores our bones, joints, muscles, and other connective
tissues and how they grow, with sixty hands-on games, experiments,
and activities.
    ISBN 1-55652-367-X
    1. Musculoskeletal system—Experiments Juvenile literature.
2. Human growth—Experiments Juvenile literature. [1. Muscular
system Experiments.   2. Skeleton Experiments.   3. Growth
Experiments.   4. Experiments.] I. Title.
QP301.025 1999
612.7—dc21   99-20864
                                                      CIP

Design and illustrations: © 1999 by Fran Lee

© 1999 by Michelle O'Brien-Palmer
All rights reserved
Published by Chicago Review Press, Incorporated
814 North Franklin Street
Chicago, Illinois 60610
ISBN-13: 978-1-55652-367-0
ISBN-10: 1-55652-367-X

Printed in the United States of America
5 4 3 2

Watch Me Grow is respectfully and lovingly dedicated to my professors,
Dr. Betty Matthews and the late **Dr. Elta May Mast** (Sis).
They taught their students to facilitate learning through interesting,
relevant, and purposeful curriculum based upon the needs of the learner.
Betty and Sis enriched the lives of their students and all of those served by their students.

Contents

Introduction for Parents and Teachers

Watch Me Grow is all about the musculoskeletal system. It explores our building blocks (cells), framework (bones), movements (muscles), and connections (joints, tendons, and ligaments). Children will be introduced to basic measurement, simple plotting, pattern graphing, recording findings in scientific diaries, and much more. Each activity is designed to be fun and simple and to promote learning by engaging children in a process of self-discovery. Even young children become scientists as they predict outcomes, gather materials, make scientific observations, and respond to their findings. Learning about the wonders of the amazing musculoskeletal system through these hands-on activities provides instant information and introduces children to the scientific process of discovery that they will use in their scientific inquiries for the rest of their lives.

The format used in each *Watch Me Grow* activity is purposeful. It reflects the progression used in any scientific exploration. The basic concepts have been preserved as children are transitioned into the process of discovery using language that is familiar to them. Each activity begins with the phrase "Did you know?," which corresponds to research and new information. "You will need" introduces children to the materials needed to conduct their experiments. With the phrase "What do you think?" every activity allows the child to make an outcome prediction, or hypothesis. "Now you are ready to" explains the procedure one would follow in testing the hypothesis. The "Brain exercise" gives children an opportunity to draw conclusions from their scientific observations.

Each chapter begins with a poem that can be sung to a familiar tune. Potentially new words from the chapter are defined in the "Wonderful Words" page. The topic being explored is discussed in "My Body at Work." Journal sheets are provided in each chapter to help children record and reflect as they connect language, artwork, and learning. Make as many copies as you need.

The last section references lively, fact-filled nonfiction books that will help you delve even further into the topics covered by the activities. This section also features a list of recommended products, the manufacturer's address, and current (as of printing) prices.

All activities have been field-tested successfully in

homes and classrooms. Most require simple materials that can be easily adjusted to accommodate your children. In these cases exact quantities of materials have not been specified. Estimated yields are given for the baking activity.

Initially, all of the activities will require adult supervision. After completing the activities together, many teachers and parents choose to set up learning centers using some of the activity materials on the topic being explored. This is a great way to extend and expand learning.

Watch Me Grow is an exploration of self. As children explore each facet of their musculoskeletal system, they will be fascinated by the intricacies of their bodies. They'll learn what it really means to be "double-jointed," and where the smallest bones, muscles, and joints are found in their bodies. Cell cookies and making fun data doors will introduce them to the three basic components of a cell. Their thirst for new knowledge and new tongue-twisting language will be hard to quench.

Nothing is more interesting to most of us than understanding how our bodies work. Join your children as you reexplore the wonders of your amazing body!

Grow, Grow, Grow

Watch Me Grow

On top of my forehead
I'm covered with cells.
They make up my stomach
and kidneys as well.

Cells are the building blocks
Of all living things.
They need the nutrition
that good eating brings.

My body has trillions
To help me each day.
They make me grow taller,
They change what I weigh.

I'm learning to measure
And read a scale too.
So I can tell how much
My body just grew!

Sung to "On Top of Old Smoky"

In Grow, Grow, Grow you will find

Wonderful Words from Grow, Grow, Grow

Bar Graph
A bar graph is a quick way to share information and patterns using columns.

Cell
All living things are made up of cells. Cells are the basic structures of all living things.

Cell Membrane
This is the wall that keeps the cell together. Cell membranes let in food and let out waste.

Cell Nucleus
The nucleus is the brain of the cell. A cell nucleus is near the center of a cell and controls cell activities.

Mitochondria
Mitochondria are the powerhouses of a cell. They produce energy for the cell.

Nutritionist
A nutritionist is a person who studies what our bodies need to eat to stay healthy and grow.

Plot-a-Point Graph
Individual points are plotted and connected to share information and show patterns in a plot-a-point graph.

Cell

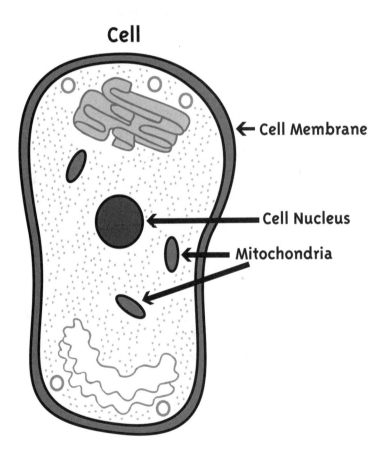

← Cell Membrane

← Cell Nucleus

← Mitochondria

My Body at Work

What should I know about how I grow?

✪ You began your life as one tiny cell. All living things are made up of cells. They are the smallest structures in all living things. Most cells are so small, they can only be seen under a microscope.

✪ A cell nucleus is found near the center of a cell and acts like a brain. The cell membrane lets food in and wastes out. The mighty mitochondria are the energy source for your cells. You are made up of billions of cells!

✪ Each cell has a very special job. Some cells become heart cells and some cells become blood cells. There are muscle cells, bone cells, and skin cells, too. Cells that are alike come together to make tissues. Different types of tissue work together to make organs like your heart or your skin.

✪ Your cells grow all of your life. Your body sheds thousands of dead skin cells every minute. In about one month's time, every one of your skin cells has been replaced by a new cell.

✪ Living things need good nutrition and water for life. Plants need sunshine, water, and nutrition. You need good food to eat, plenty of water to drink, daily exercise, and family and friends to love you and care for you.

✪ Scientists record their observations in pictures and words. As you observe plants, your friends, and yourself growing, it will be important to record your observations in a diary. You can take the information you learn and make fun graphs to share with others.

My Grow, Grow, Grow Journal

Today I learned

1 How Does Your Garden Grow?

Did you know?
Plants need food, water, and sunlight to grow.

You will need
2 very small, healthy indoor plants (no more than 2 inches tall)

Marker

Label

Camera (optional)

See and Draw Observation Diary from activity #2, I'm a Scientist! Observation Diaries, page 12

See and Measure Observation Diary from activity #2, I'm a Scientist! Observation Diaries, page 13

2 water trays

Closet

Water

What do you think?
If I give a healthy plant sunlight, food, and the right amount of water, it (will) or (won't) grow.

Now you are ready to
1. Label the plants #1 and #2. If convenient, take pictures of the plants.
2. Turn to activity #2, I'm a Scientist! Observation Diaries, page 11, and complete steps 1–6 before going on with activity #1.
3. Place a water tray under the pot of plant #1 and place it in a sunny spot.
4. Place plant #2 in a dark closet. What do you think will happen to a plant that is not watered or exposed to sunlight?
5. Water plant #1 once a day for 7 days. Leave plant #2 in the closet.
6. On the seventh day, take plant #2 out of the closet. Turn to activity #2, I'm a Scientist! Observation Diaries, page 11, and complete steps 7–10. How have the two plants changed?
7. Place plant #2 in a sunny spot near plant #1. Put a water tray under plant #2 and give it water. Give plant #2 water.Do you think it will grow now, or has it been in the closet too long? Water it for the next week and see what happens.

Brain exercise

When plants go without water and sunlight, . . .

Body Note

Just like the plants, in order to stay healthy we need to take good care of our bodies.

Key to Success

The plants you purchase must be very healthy.

Hint

Depending on the needs of your particular type of plant, it may or may not survive the week without water and sunshine.

Did you know?

Scientists record their scientific findings in pictures and words.

You will need

Plants #1 and #2 from activity #1, How Does Your Garden Grow?, page 9

See and Draw Observation Diary, page 12, copied onto white paper

See and Measure Observation Diary, page 13, copied onto white paper

Pencil

Ruler or yardstick

Colored pencils

Now you are ready to

1. With the pencil, write your name at the top of each Observation Diary.
2. Observe plant #1 on the first day.
3. What do you see? Draw what you see in the first box of the See and Draw Observation Diary for plant #1, using colored pencils or markers.
4. Measure plant #1 with the ruler by folding the ruler at the 0 line, placing the bottom of the ruler on top of the soil, and reading up. Read at the closest half-inch to the plant's height.
5. Color to the closest half-inch on the first ruler of the See and Measure Observation Diary for plant #1.
6. Now complete steps 1–5 for plant #2.
7. Observe plant #1 on the seventh day.
8. What do you see? Draw what you see in the second box of the See and Draw Observation Diary for plant #1.
9. Measure plant #1. Color in the number of inches on the second ruler of the See and Measure Observation Diary for plant #1.
10. Repeat steps 7–9 with plant #2.

See and Draw Observation Diary

My Name_____

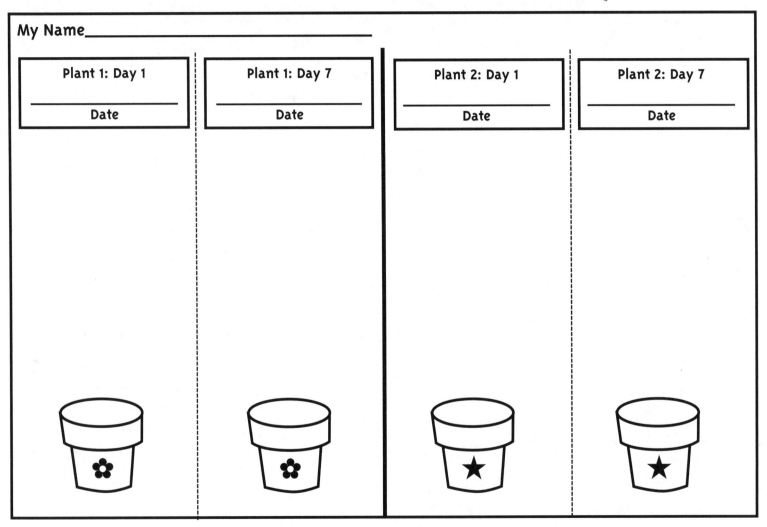

Plant 1: Day 1	Plant 1: Day 7	Plant 2: Day 1	Plant 2: Day 7
_____	_____	_____	_____
Date	Date	Date	Date

See and Measure Observation Diary

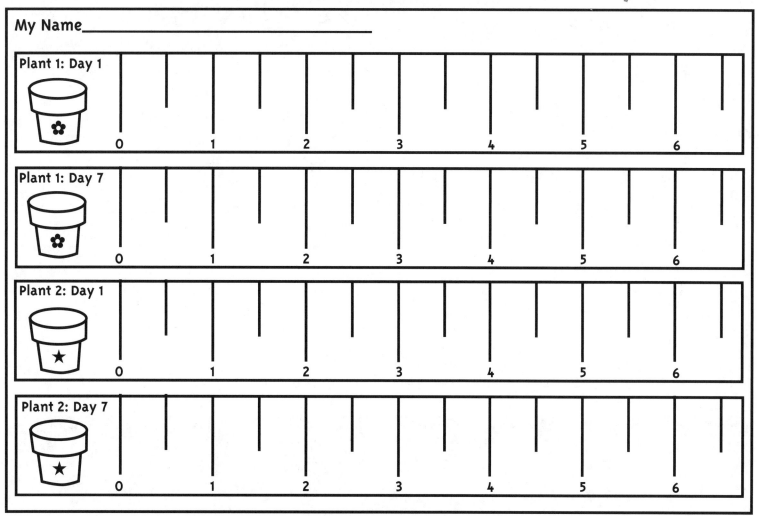

My Name _____

Plant 1: Day 1

0   1   2   3   4   5   6

Plant 1: Day 7

0   1   2   3   4   5   6

Plant 2: Day 1

0   1   2   3   4   5   6

Plant 2: Day 7

0   1   2   3   4   5   6

3 Plot-a-Plant Predictions

Did you know?

Plants each grow at their own special pace, just as you do.

You will need

Amaryllis plant (already potted)
Plot-a-Plant Graph, page 15, copied onto white card stock
Pencil
Ruler or yardstick

What do you think?

If I water the amaryllis plant and place it in a sunny spot, it will grow to be _____ inches tall in 7 weeks.

Now you are ready to

1. Write your prediction on how tall the amaryllis plant will grow in 7 weeks on the back of the Plot-a-Plant Graph.

2. Place the plant in a nice sunny spot. Water it according to the directions.

3. Use the ruler to measure the plant from the soil up.

4. Record the plant's starting height with a dot on your Plot-a-Plant Graph.

5. Measure the plant once a week for 6 weeks. Record its growth with a dot on your graph.

6. At the end of 7 weeks, connect all the dots. This is your plant's growth pattern. Check your prediction on the back of your graph to see how close your prediction matched the plant's actual height.

Brain exercise

The amaryllis plant grew . . .

Activity Goals	Body Note	Key to Success	Hint
To observe and record growth over time. To learn how to plot points on a graph.	Some people grow quickly and others grow at a more even pace. It is hard to predict how fast we will grow.	Patience is required for the first couple of weeks. This plant starts out slowly and then speeds up its growth.	To extend this activity, try measuring in centimeters, or create your own unit of measurement.

Plot-a-Plant Graph

Inches						
15						
14						
13						
12						
11						
10						
9						
8						
7						
6						
5						
4						
3						
2						
1						
0	1	2	3	4	5	6	7

Week Number

Watch Me Grow, © 1999. Published by Chicago Review Press, Inc., 800-888-7471.

4 Food for Growth—Make a Pyramid Stand

Did you know?

Nutritionists are people who study what foods help keep us healthy. They have created a food pyramid to help you eat the right amount of different kinds of nutritious foods.

You will need

Pyramid Stand design, page 17, copied onto colored card stock

Scissors

Colored markers or pencils

Now you are ready to

1. Cut out the square pyramid design. Color in the food drawings.
2. Fold the square on the dotted line to form a pyramid shape.
3. Place the pyramid on your desk or in your kitchen so that you can see the different food groups.
4. Flip your pyramid over to see how many daily servings you need to eat of each type of food.

Activity Goal	Body Note	Key to Success	Hint
To make a fun nutrition guide using the national nutrition standards.	Fats, oils, and sweets should be used sparingly.	Talk with the children about the foods in each of the food categories and the daily serving guidelines before they make their pyramids. Use the pyramids to evaluate their meals with them.	Some children may need help with cutting and folding. Keep the pyramids in a location close to where they eat for reference purposes.

Pyramid Stand

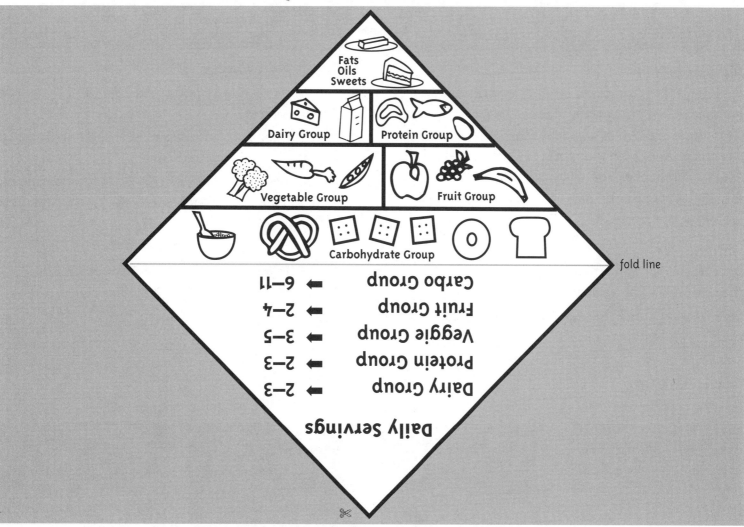

Fats
Oils
Sweets

Dairy Group

Protein Group

Vegetable Group

Fruit Group

Carbohydrate Group

fold line

Carbo Group ⬅ 6–11
Fruit Group ⬅ 2–4
Veggie Group ⬅ 3–5
Protein Group ⬅ 2–3
Dairy Group ⬅ 2–3

Daily Servings

Data Doors—The Parts of a Cell

Did you know?

All living things are made up of cells. Cells have a number of structures within them. The most important structure is the nucleus, which is the brain of the cell. It controls the cell. Other important structures are the "mighty" mitochondria. They are the powerhouses of the cell. Every cell also has a cell membrane, which lets food in and wastes out.

You will need

Data Doors: The Parts of a Cell, page 19, copied onto the bottom half of a sheet of card stock

Data Doors Paste-On Stickers, page 20, copied onto a sheet of white paper

Scissors

Glue or paste

Colored markers

Now you are ready to

1. Fold the card stock in half so that the Data Doors title is on the outside.

2. Cut along the 2 dotted lines only to the top of the fold line to make the Data Doors.

3. Cut out the Data Doors Paste-On Stickers and glue or paste each sticker onto the card stock under the Data Door that has its name.

4. Color the Data Doors and the stickers if you like.

5. Lift the Data Doors and test what you know about the parts of a cell and what jobs they do.

Activity Goal	Body Note	Key to Success	Hint
To learn the basic cell structures.	You began your life as one tiny cell.	Discuss the three basic parts of the cell with the child or children before you start the activity.	Do this activity before activity #6, Cellular Delights Cookie Recipe, page 21.

Data Doors: The Parts of a Cell

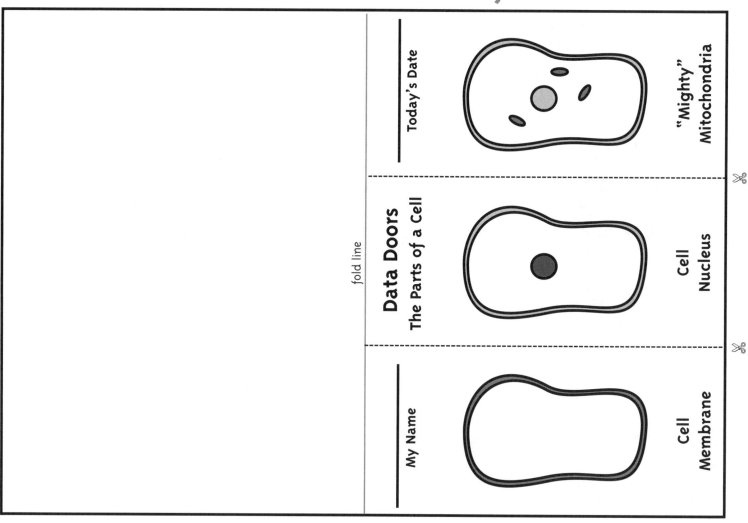

Today's Date

"Mighty" Mitochondria

fold line

Data Doors
The Parts of a Cell

Cell Nucleus

My Name

Cell Membrane

Data Doors Paste-On Stickers

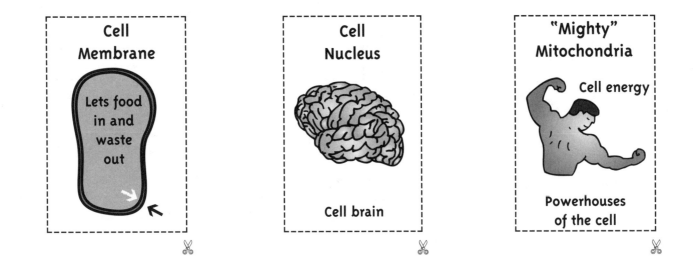

Cell
Membrane

Lets food
in and
waste
out

Cell
Nucleus

Cell brain

"Mighty"
Mitochondria

Cell energy

Powerhouses
of the cell

6 Cellular Delights Cookie Recipe

You will need

2½ cups flour
1 teaspoon baking soda
1 teaspoon cream of tartar
1½ cups powdered sugar
1 cup softened butter
1 egg
1 teaspoon vanilla extract
½ teaspoon almond extract
Wooden spoon
Measuring cups
Measuring spoons
Medium bowl
Large mixing bowl
Electric mixer (adult supervision is required)
Lightly floured pastry cloth
Rolling pin
Lightly greased baking sheet
Oven
Plastic spatula
Cookie cutter (round or oval)

Makes approximately three dozen 4-inch cookies

Now you are ready to

1. Measure and pour the flour, baking soda, and cream of tartar into the medium bowl. Mix these ingredients together with a wooden spoon. Set aside.

2. Measure the powdered sugar and pour it into the large mixing bowl. Place the softened butter in with the sugar. Blend these ingredients together with the electric mixer until they are smooth.

3. Measure and add the egg, vanilla extract, and almond extract to the sugar mixture. Mix them together until they are smooth.

4. Add half the dry ingredients from the medium mixing bowl to the sugar mixture. Mix until well blended.

5. Pour the rest of the dry ingredients into the large mixing bowl with the sugar mixture. Blend the mixture until smooth.

6. Place the dough in the refrigerator for 2 to 3 hours before baking.

7. When you are ready to cut the cookies, set the oven to 375°F.

8. Roll out the dough on the pastry sheet. Cut each cookie with a round or oval cookie cutter.

9. Follow the decorating directions in activity #7, Decorate Your Cellular Delights, on page 23.

10. After decorating the cookies, place them on a lightly greased baking sheet and bake them at 375°F for 9 to 10 minutes.

Decorate Your Cellular Delights

You will need

Cookie recipe, pages 21–22
Round, flat-bottomed candies, like small gumdrops
Good & Plenty candies
Thin strings of red licorice
Clean pair of scissors (washed with soap and hot water)
Camera (optional)

Now you are ready to

1. Follow the cookie recipe on pages 21–22 up to step 9.
2. Place one flat-bottomed gumdrop in the center of each cookie. This is your cell nucleus—the brain of your cookie cell. Place three or four Good & Plenty candies in different places on the cookie. These are mitochondria—the powerhouses of your cell. Place the licorice string around the outside of your cookie and cut it with the scissors when you get it to the right length. This is your cookie's cell membrane.
3. Go back to step 10 in the cookie recipe and wait for your Cellular Delights to bake.
4. Take a picture of your special cookies and let them cool down. Enjoy your cookies!

Activity Goal	Body Note	Key to Success	Hint
To participate in a hands-on activity that teaches the basic parts of a cell.	These cookies were made to look like animal cells. Plant cells have a more rectangular shape.	Each child makes his or her own cell cookie. Stick the points of the licorice into the cookie to secure them. Gently push the gumdrops and candies into the cookie dough. If you are working with a large group, cut the licorice before decorating.	Children never forget these cookies or the basic parts of the cell. If you are in a hurry, substitute chilled sugar cookie dough from the grocery store. As children get older, add other parts of cells to the cookies.

⑧ See-a-Cell? Look Inside

Did you know?
Cells are the smallest structures of all living things. They are considered to be the building blocks of life.

You will need
1 orange, cut in half and stored in a resealable plastic bag

Magnifying glass or 30X microscope (see product information, page 137)

Paper towels

What do you think?
I (will) or (won't) be able to see the orange's cells.

Now you are ready to
1. Look at the cut orange. What do you see? The juice ran out of the cells when the cell membrane of the orange was cut. The fibers you see are the cells of the orange.
2. Use the magnifying glass or microscope to take a closer look at the cells.
3. When you are finished observing the cells of the orange, you can eat it or use it to make orange juice.

Brain exercise
When the orange was cut, . . .

Activity Goal	Body Note	Key to Success	Hint
To see plant cells up close.	Your cells have membranes around them for protection. The cell membrane lets nutrition in and wastes out of the cell.	Each child needs to be able to get a close look at the orange. A magnifying glass will work, but the 30X portable microscope works very well.	This activity can get messy. It is important to have paper towels or napkins available for the children.

9 Body Outlines—All Shapes and Sizes

Did you know?
We all grow to be different shapes and sizes.

You will need
2 large sheets butcher paper (each large enough to hold a body outline)

Pencil

Markers

Partner

Camera

File folder labeled "All About Me"

Yardstick

Now you are ready to
1. Place the butcher paper on a clean, uncarpeted floor. Select a partner.

2. Carefully, lie down on the paper and ask your partner to draw a line around your body with the pencil.

3. Using markers, write your name at the top of the paper outline.

4. Fill in the details by drawing in your face and clothing.

5. Take a picture of your body outline and place it in your "All About Me" file folder.

6. For fun, practice measuring by using the yardstick to measure your arm length from your shoulder to your hand.

7. Repeat steps 1 and 2, drawing your partner's outline.

8. Look at the differences between your outlines.

Brain exercise
I liked my outline because . . .

TOMMY

Emily

Rex

Activity Goal

To create a full-size body outline.

Body Note

Each of us is a unique shape and size.

Key to Success

Wearing tight-fitting clothing produces the most accurate outline.

Hint

Children like to cut out body outlines and display them on bedroom or classroom walls. It's fun to make a new outline in six months and compare the two outlines.

You will need

2 sheets (8½ x 11 inches) bright-colored construction paper

2 sheets (8½ x 11 inches) white construction paper

Pencil

Your foot (in a sock)

Partner

Your hand

Scissors

Glue

"All About Me" file folder

Now you are ready to

1. Take your right shoe off. Place one sheet of colored construction paper on a flat, uncarpeted surface. Carefully step onto it, keeping most of your weight on your other foot.

2. Ask your partner to draw the outline of your foot by tracing around it on the paper.

3. Put your shoe back on your foot. Cut out the line you've drawn.

4. Write your name and the date on your foot outline.

5. Place your hand on the other sheet of colored construction paper.

6. Trace around your hand on the paper.

7. Cut out the line you've drawn.

8. Glue your foot outline to a sheet of white construction paper and label the paper "My Footprint." Write your name and the date on the paper.

9. Glue your hand outline to the other sheet of white construction paper and label the paper "My Handprint." Write your name and the date on the paper and place it in your "All About Me" file folder.

Activity Goal	Body Note	Key to Success	Hint
To make a template of each child's hand and foot for future comparison.	Each person grows at his or her own pace.	Adult supervision and help may be required for tracing, cutting, and pasting.	A hard, flat surface like a desk works well for tracing hands. The floor works well for tracing feet.

11   How We Measure Up Height Bar Graph

You will need

1 sheet (4 feet long) colored butcher paper

1 sheet (30 inches x 36 inches) Post-it graph easel paper (plain graph easel paper works well, too)

3 small footprint cutouts (design your own or use die cuts)

Yardstick

Pencil

Marker

Glue

Scissors

Now you are ready to

1. Lay out the butcher paper on a flat, clean surface.

2. Measure 6 inches down from the top of the butcher paper. Draw a line across the paper in pencil.

3. Measure 5 inches in from the left edge of the paper. Draw a line down the left margin in pencil.

4. Match up the top left corner of the easel paper with the pencil lines drawn on the butcher paper.

5. Rub the top of the easel paper to keep it attached to the butcher paper.

6. Glue the edges of the easel paper onto the butcher paper.

7. Write measurements on the butcher paper, leaving as much space as possible on the left margin (footprint cutouts will be inserted at the 3-foot, 4-foot, and 5-foot marks). Start labeling the graph grid moving from the bottom of the graph paper up. Each horizontal row is 1 inch wide. Label the bottom row 2'6''. The next row up will be 2'7'', and so on, until you get to the top of the grid.

8. Glue a footprint cutout to the left of the 3-foot, 4-foot, and 5-foot marks. Label the footprints.

9. Using a marker, write "How We Measure Up"across the top of your butcher paper.

10. Find a place to hang your graph. Place the top of the graph 6 feet up from the floor. Once hung, it should be 2 feet from the floor at the bottom, so that the first measurement on the graph is accurate.

How We Measure Up

Measurement: Height

5'6"
5'5"
5'4"
5'3"
5'2"
5'1"
5'
4'11"
4'10"
4'9"
4'8"
4'7"
4'6"
4'5"
4'4"
4'3"
4'2"
4'1"
4'
3'11"
3'10"
3'9"
3'8"
3'7"
3'6"
3'5"
3'4"
3'3"
3'2"
3'1"
3'
2'11"
2'10"
2'9"
2'8"
2'7"
2'6"

Person Measured

12 Let's Graph It!

Did you know?

At the age of seven, you are about 75 percent of your adult height.

You will need

How We Measure Up height bar graph, page 28, hanging on wall

Partner

Ruler

Pencil

Markers

My Height Graph, page 33, and Our Height Bar Graph, page 32, copied onto white paper

"All About Me" file folder

What do you think?

If my partner measures my height, I will be about _____ feet tall.

Now you are ready to

1. Stand up next to the How We Measure Up bar graph. Turn around and back up until the heels of your feet touch the wall.

2. Stand as straight as you can.

3. Ask your partner to place a flat ruler on top of your head and mark your height in one of the columns on the graph (each column is 1 inch wide).

4. Use your favorite colored marker to trace your height line, and make a 1-inch-wide solid column going down the graph paper. Write your name inside the column.

5. Measure each of your friends, using a 1-inch-wide column per person. You can use this graph to measure up to 25 friends.

6. Each person measured can record his or her own height on the My Height Graph, page 33.

7. Pass around the Our Height Bar Graph, page 32, so that each person can record his or her height in a column. Ask an adult to make a copy of this completed graph for each person.

8. Place your graphs in your "All About Me" file folder. Measure each other again every month or two months and record your growth on the individual and group height graphs.

Activity Goals

To practice measurement skills and to introduce the concept of graphing.

Body Note

Depending on our parents and grandparents, we all grow to be different heights.

Key to Success

Adult supervision is required. The butcher-paper How We Measure Up bar graph has to be straight-cut at the top and bottom for it to accurately reflect height. Accurate, level placement on the wall is vital.

Hint

An adult needs to teach the children how to measure each other.

Our Height Bar Graph

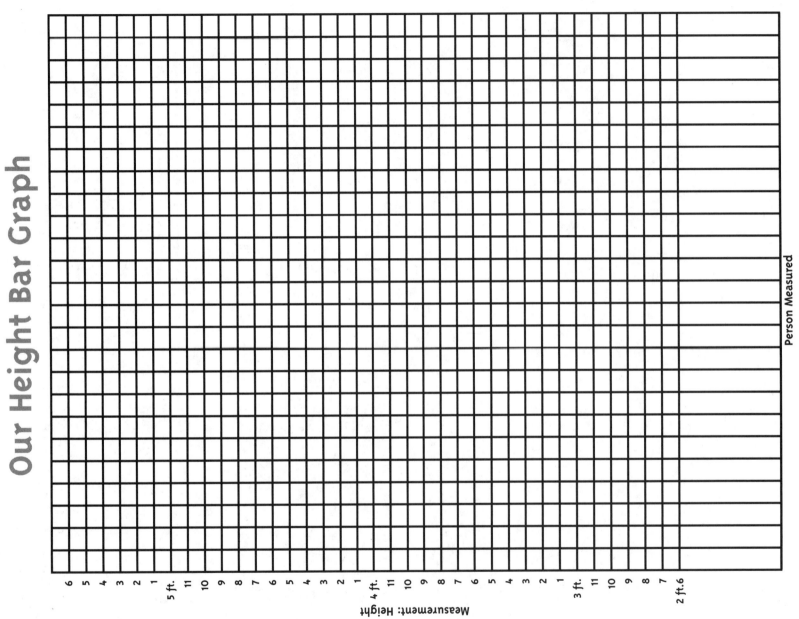

Measurement: Height

Person Measured

My Height Graph

My Name _____

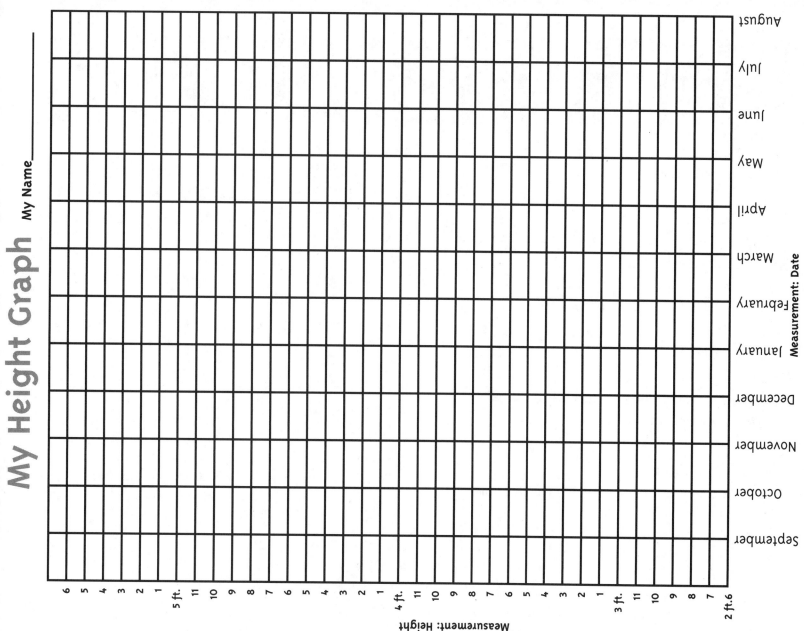

Measurement: Height

Measurement: Date

September · October · November · December · January · February · March · April · May · June · July · August

6 · 5 · 4 · 3 · 2 · 1 · 5 ft. · 11 · 10 · 9 · 8 · 7 · 6 · 5 · 4 · 3 · 2 · 1 · 4 ft. · 11 · 10 · 9 · 8 · 7 · 6 · 5 · 4 · 3 · 2 · 1 · 3 ft. · 11 · 10 · 9 · 8 · 7 · 2 ft.6

Watch Me Grow, © 1999. Published by Chicago Review Press, Inc., 800-888-7471.

13 Weight Wheel—Take a Spin

Did you know?
We measure our weight in pounds.

You will need
My Weight Wheel, pages 36 and 37, copied onto colored card stock

Scissors

X-Acto knife (for adult use only)

Bradley clip

Bathroom scale

Pencil

My Weight Graph, page 38, copied onto white paper

"All About Me" file folder

What do you think?
If I stand on a bathroom scale, I will weigh about
_____ pounds.

Now you are ready to
1. Cut out the front and back sides of My Weight Wheel.
2. Place the circles back to back, so that the writing shows on both sides. Ask an adult to cut a very small x in the center of both circles of the weight wheel, cutting over the black center dot.
3. Push the bradley clip through the two circles and fasten it by folding it behind the back circle.
4. Stand on the bathroom scale. Look down to see what the scale says you weigh. If you can't read it, get an adult to help you.
5. Write your weight and the date under the right month on your weight wheel.
6. Weigh yourself once a month to see how your weight changes over time.
7. Plot your weight on the My Weight Graph, page 38. Place your weight wheel and your graph in your "All About Me" file folder.

Brain exercise
When I stepped on the scale, I . . .

Activity Goal

To practice measuring body weight and recording the information on a graph.

Body Note

Our weight changes a little bit every day.

Key to Success

Teach children how to use a bathroom scale before this activity.

Hint

Plot the first point on the graph for the child so that he knows how to do it the next time.

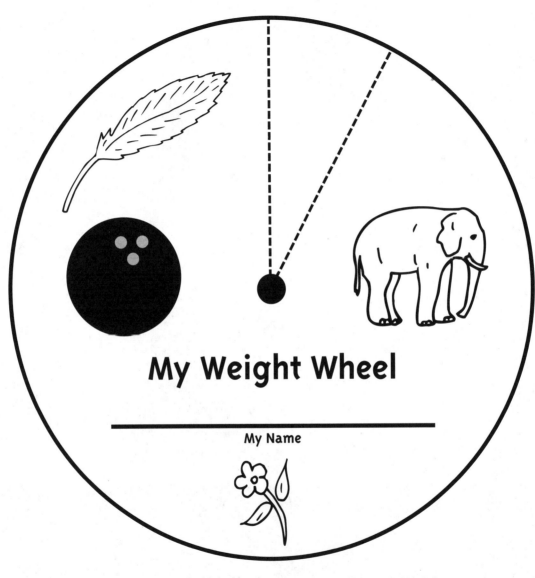

My Weight Wheel

_____
My Name

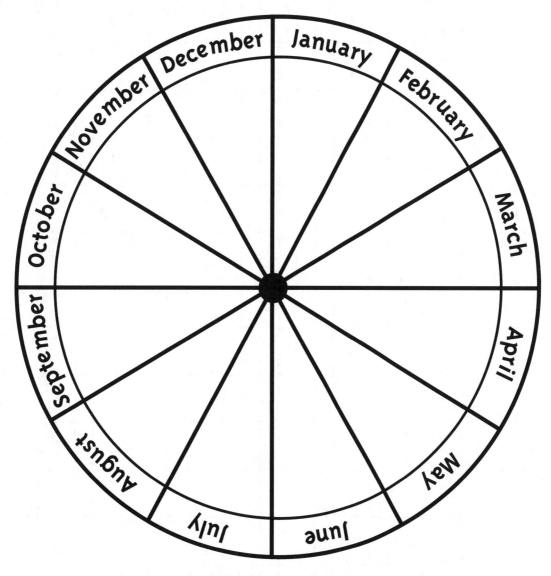

My Weight Graph

My Name _____

Measurement: Weight

	September	October	November	December	January	February	March	April	May	June	July	August
85												
84												
83												
82												
81												
80												
79												
78												
77												
76												
75												
74												
73												
72												
71												
70												
69												
68												
67												
66												
65												
64												
63												
62												
61												
60												
59												
58												
57												
56												
55												
54												
53												
52												
51												
50												
49												

Measurement: Date

Watch Me Grow, © 1999. Published by Chicago Review Press, Inc., 800-888-7471.

14 All About Me—My Growth Portfolio

You will need

1-inch ring binder with pockets

1 plastic see-through pocket, hole-punched for the binder

Photograph of your body outline (optional)

3-hole punch

Your handprint from the activity on page 27

Your footprint from the activity on page 27

Our Height Bar Graph, page 32

My Height Graph, page 33

My Weight Graph, page 38

My Weight Wheel, page 36

Add later:

My Bones Grow! Sheet, My Muscles Grow! Sheet

Now you are ready to

1. Open up the notebook and place your see-through pocket inside.
2. Put the photograph of your body outline in the pocket (optional).
3. Hole-punch all the remaining sheets except My Weight Wheel, and place them in the notebook.
4. Put your weight wheel in the inside pocket of your notebook.
5. Decorate the outside of the notebook with stickers and markers and label it "All About Me."
6. Keep this notebook in a safe place so that you can record new information once a month or as often as you would like.

Activity Goal

To collect body information and organize it for future reference.

Body Note

It is interesting to watch how our bodies change over time.

Key to Success

Help children to collect and hole-punch their information.

Hint

Keep the notebook in a safe place so that it is easy to pull out in the future. Set a monthly date like the first day of the month or the birthday day of the month to gather new information.

Bundle of Bones

My Bones Song

I'll be wearing all my bones, when I come (creak, creak)!
I'll be wearing all my bones, when I come!
I'll be wearing all my bones.
If I don't, I won't be known.
I'd be jelly on my own, without my bones (squeak, squeak)!

Well, my bones are quite fantastic, yes they are (ya-hoo)!
Well, my bones are quite fantastic, yes they are!
Well, my bones are quite fantastic.
If they weren't quite so elastic
I could not do my gymnastics any more (boo, hoo)!

Yes, my bones need calcium phosphate, so they'll grow (uh, huh)!
Yes, my bones need calcium phosphate, so they'll grow!
Yes, my bones need calcium phosphate
Or they'd never cal-ci-fi-cate.
Rubber bones are not that great a fate (oh, no)!

Oh, I exercise and eat three meals each day (sure do)!
Oh, I exercise and eat three meals each day!
Oh, I exercise and eat three meals
So my bones are as strong as steel.
I really like how good I feel each day (hurray)!

"Sung to "She'll Be Coming 'Round the Mountain"

In Bundle of Bones you will find

Wonderful Words About My Bundle of Bones

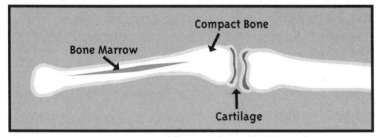

Bone Marrow Bones are filled with a jellylike substance called bone marrow. Bone marrow makes up to five billion red blood cells a day. It also makes some types of white blood cells and stores fat.

Calcium Phosphate The mineral calcium phosphate gives your bones their strength.

Cartilage Cartilage is the rubbery substance found at the tip of your nose, on the tops of your ears, on bones, and in between the vertebrae in your back.

Collagen Collagen is a protein found in bone. It gives bone the ability to bend.

Compact Bone The outside of your bones is called compact bone. It is the second-hardest material in your body. The enamel in your teeth is the hardest material.

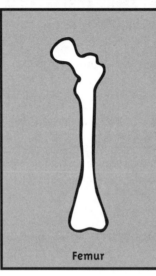

Femur

Femur Your femur is the largest and strongest bone in your body. It is located in your upper leg.

Vertebrae The 26 bones that make up your backbone and protect your spinal cord are called vertebrae (singular, vertebra).

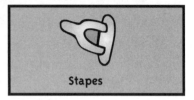

Stapes

Stapes The smallest bone in your body, the stapes is one of three small bones found in each of your ears. "Stapes" means "stirrup" in Latin. Can you see why?

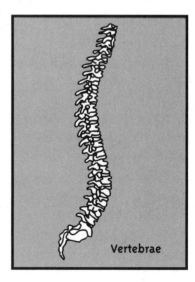

Vertebrae

44

My Body at Work

What should I know about my bones?

✪ Your bones are alive. They give you your shape and strength and support your body. Without this bony framework, you would be shapeless. Your skeleton helps to protect your heart, lungs, and other organs. Your skull protects your brain. You have 26 vertebrae making up your backbone. Your vertebrae protect your nerves and make it possible for you to bend, roll, and twist. Another word for backbone is spine. Bones are filled with a jellylike substance. It's called bone marrow. Blood cells are made in your bone marrow. Your bones are amazing!

✪ You were born with more than 300 bones. Your bones will grow together so that eventually, when you are an adult, you will have about 206 bones. Right now, you have more bones in your body than your parents do, and your bones heal faster than their bones.

✪ At birth your bones were soft. They were made out of cartilage, which is the rubbery substance found at the tip of your nose. As you grew, your bones went through a process of calcification. This is when your body coated your bones with a mineral called calcium phosphate. Calcium is found in milk. It helps to build strong bones.

✪ Bone is stronger for its weight than steel or reinforced concrete. Many of your bones have a cylinder-like shape. A cylinder is one of the strongest forms in nature.

✪ Bones are held together by joints, ligaments, and muscles. You will learn about them later in this book.

✪ Long bones are found in your arms, legs, and fingers. They are skinny with swollen ends. Short bones are found in your feet and wrists. They are wider and thicker than long bones. Flat bones like your ribs and shoulder blades have platelike shapes. Irregular bones come in all shapes and sizes, from tiny ear bones to the flat, rounded bones in your back, called vertebrae.

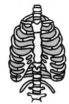

My Bundle of Bones Journal

Today I learned

① Best Guess—Bone Trivia Cards

Did you know?

You were born with more than 300 bones. Your bones will eventually grow together to make about 206 bones.

You will need

2 sheets (8 x 11 inches) card stock

Bone Trivia card fronts, page 49, copied onto one sheet of card stock

Bone Trivia card backs, page 50, copied onto the other sheet of card stock

Scissors

Glue

Partner (one partner needs to be able to read)

Rubber band

What do you think?

If I try to guess the answers for the bone trivia questions, I will guess_____ out of 4 correctly.

Now you are ready to

1. Cut out the 16 Bone Trivia cards from both sheets of card stock.

2. Match the question fronts to their answer backs. Glue the matching card pieces together, back to back. Laminate if you like.

3. Place the cards with the question side up.

4. Ask your partner to give a best-guess answer to the first four questions. If one of you can't read, the partner who can read should read each question aloud. Once a question is answered, check the back of the card to see if it was answered correctly. How well did your partner guess?

5. Next, it is your turn to guess the answers to questions 5–8. How well did you guess? When you are finished, place a rubber band around the cards so they don't get lost.

6. Try answering the questions again. See how many you can get right this time. Over time you'll be surprised at how much you know about your bones.

Brain exercise

When I guessed the answers, I . . .

Activity Goal	Body Note	Key to Success	Hint
To learn new information about bones in a fun trivia card game.	Some people have more bones than others.	One partner needs to be able to read. Children may need help with cutting out the cards.	Children love playing with the trivia cards. It is a fun challenge for them to test their knowledge over and over.

Bone Trivia Card Fronts

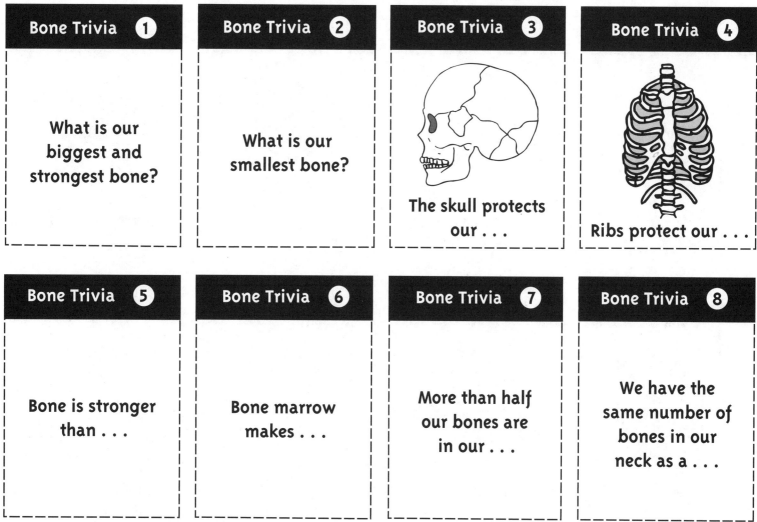

Bone Trivia ①	Bone Trivia ②	Bone Trivia ③	Bone Trivia ④
What is our biggest and strongest bone?	What is our smallest bone?	The skull protects our . . .	Ribs protect our . . .

Bone Trivia ⑤	Bone Trivia ⑥	Bone Trivia ⑦	Bone Trivia ⑧
Bone is stronger than . . .	Bone marrow makes . . .	More than half our bones are in our . . .	We have the same number of bones in our neck as a . . .

Bone Trivia Card Backs

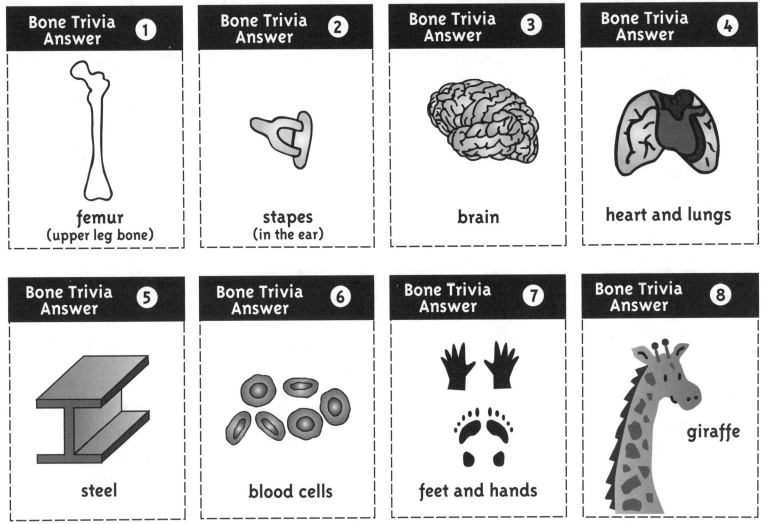

Bone Trivia Answer 1

femur
(upper leg bone)

Bone Trivia Answer 2

stapes
(in the ear)

Bone Trivia Answer 3

brain

Bone Trivia Answer 4

heart and lungs

Bone Trivia Answer 5

steel

Bone Trivia Answer 6

blood cells

Bone Trivia Answer 7

feet and hands

Bone Trivia Answer 8

giraffe

Watch Me Grow, © 1999. Published by Chicago Review Press, Inc., 800-888-7471.

② Brittle Bones? No Elasticity

Did you know?
Collagen is a substance found in bones. Collagen makes bones more elastic and flexible.

You will need
2 chicken leg bones, cleaned and dried

1 saucepan water

1 stove (adult supervision is required)

What do you think?
If I boil a chicken bone in water, it will be (the same as) or (different than) when I first placed it in the pan.

Now you are ready to
1. Set one chicken bone aside to compare it to the boiled bone later.
2. Place the other chicken bone in a saucepan of water and heat it to boiling. Boil the chicken bone on low heat for 10 minutes.
3. Turn the stove off and let the bone cool.
4. Once the cooked bone has cooled, dry it off and compare it to the uncooked bone.
5. How are they different?

Brain exercise
When the bone was boiled, it . . .

Activity Goal	Body Note	Key to Success	Hint
To observe the effect of boiling bones.	Boiling chicken bones removes their collagen. Without collagen, the bone becomes very brittle and can break easily.	The larger the bone, the longer it must be boiled.	An adult needs to be present during this activity.

3 Knot a Bone? No Calcium

Did you know?
Without calcium phosphate, your bones wouldn't be very strong or healthy.

You will need
3 chicken leg bones, cleaned and dried
2 glass jars (including lids) filled with white vinegar
1 glass jar (including lid) filled with water
Partner

What do you think?
If I place a chicken bone in white vinegar for 1 week, it will be (the same as) or (different than) a chicken bone that I place in plain water for 1 week.

Now you are ready to
1. Pick up the bones. How do they feel? Are they soft? Are they hard? What color are they?

2. Place one chicken bone in each of the two glass jars filled with vinegar, and close the lids.

3. Place the remaining chicken bone in the water-filled glass jar, and close the lid.

4. Place the jars in a location where they will not be disturbed.

5. After 1 week, open the water-filled jar. Feel the bone. How does it feel? Try to bend it. What happens to it?

6. Next, open the jars filled with vinegar. Feel the bones. How do they feel? Try to bend them. What happens to them? Compare the bones that were soaked in vinegar. How are they the same? How are they different?

Brain exercise
When the bones sat in vinegar for 1 week, they . . .

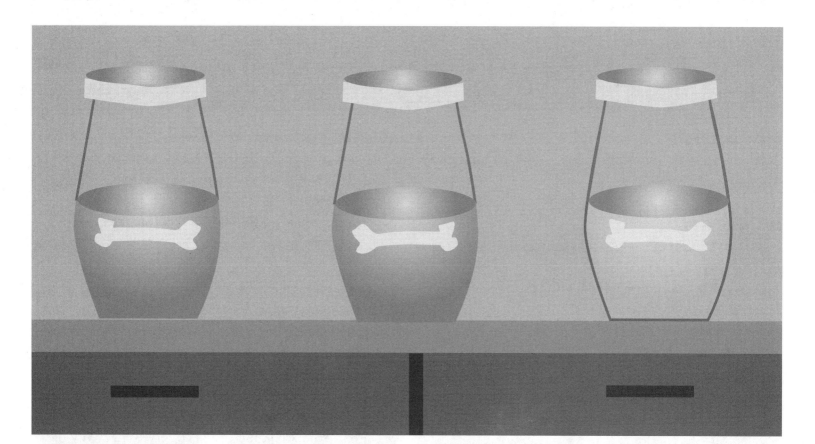

Activity Goal

To observe the effect of extracting calcium from a bone.

Body Note

White vinegar is an acid that extracts calcium from the chicken bones. This leaves the bone rubbery. Calcium provides bone strength.

Key to Success

The larger the bone, the longer it must stay in the vinegar. If you are using a particularly large bone, give this activity 2 weeks instead of 1 week.

Hint

This activity needs to be supervised, and the glass jars need to be kept in a safe location.

4 Rubbery Bone—Will Milk Fix It?

Did you know?
Calcium is a very important mineral used by your body in building healthy bones.

You will need
2 chicken leg bones previously soaked in white vinegar (see activity #3, page 52)
1 glass jar (including lid) filled with whole milk
1 empty glass jar (including lid)

What do you think?
If I place one of the rubbery chicken bones in whole milk, it will (get stronger) or (stay the same).

Now you are ready to
1. Place one of the rubbery chicken bones in the jar filled with milk, close the lid, and store it in the refrigerator.
2. Place the other rubbery chicken bone in the empty glass jar, close the lid, and store it in the refrigerator also.
3. After 1 week, open the jar containing the bone only. Feel the bone. How does it feel? Try to bend it. What happens to it?
4. Open the jar containing the bone in milk. Pour the milk out. Dry off the bone. Feel the bone. How does it feel? Try to bend it. What happens to it? Compare the two bones. Are they the same or different? Do you think the milk changed the rubbery bone? Why or why not?

Brain exercise
When the rubbery bone sat in milk for 1 week, . . .

Activity Goal

To see if a bone that has been stripped of its calcium can get back its original shape when it is soaked in milk.

Body Note

The bone is not alive. Therefore, the calcium cannot be absorbed into the bone.

Key to Success

This activity was requested unanimously by the children. They were certain that milk was the solution to rubbery bones. They hypothesized that the bone would grow, become strong again, and turn white. Ask your children to predict their own outcomes.

Hint

Many children were certain that the bone would return to its original shape because they know that milk is good for bones. It is important to allow them an opportunity to theorize why the bone didn't get stronger before you explain it.

⑤ Select-a-Shape I—Design a Rectangular Bone

Did you know?
Your bones are so strong that they can support the weight of your body.

You will need
1 index card (4 x 6 inches)
Ruler
Pencil
Scotch tape
Post-its
Several lightweight paperback books
Paper

What do you think?
If I make a hollow rectangle out of the index card, it (will) or (won't) be strong enough to hold four light-weight paperback books.

Now you are ready to
1. Make four folds, one every 1⅜ inches, along the 6-inch edge of the index card, using the ruler and a pencil to mark off the measurements. This will leave a half-inch tab at the end.
2. Use Scotch tape to tape the index card into a hollow rectangular shape. Make sure the tab overlaps on the outside. Tape it down securely.
3. Stick Post-its to the paperback books and use them to label each book #1, #2, #3, and so on.
4. Stand the hollow rectangle on one end and stack books #1–#4 on the other end one at a time, until the shape can no longer hold the books. Note the book titles and order so you can use them in activity #6, Select-a-Shape II, on page 58. What number of books could the hollow rectangle hold? Write the number on a piece of paper. Did the hollow rectangle hold more than four books?

Brain exercise
The rectangular shape . . .

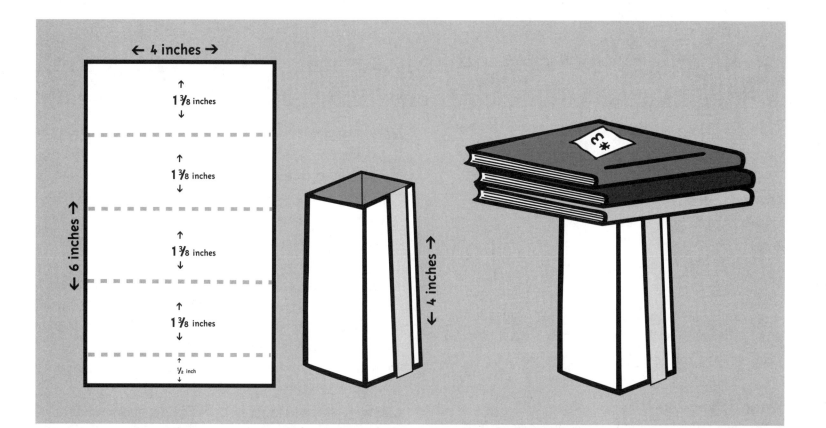

← 4 inches →

↑ 1 ⅜ inches ↓

↑ 1 ⅜ inches ↓

← 6 inches →

↑ 1 ⅜ inches ↓

↑ 1 ⅜ inches ↓

↑ ½ inch ↓

← 4 inches →

#3

Activity Goal

To test a three-dimensional rectangular shape for strength.

Body Note

The way your bones are designed makes them stronger than reinforced concrete.

Key to Success

Use only lightweight paperback books for this activity. Keep your written results to use in activity #6, Select-a-Shape II, on page 58.

Hint

If index cards aren't available, substitute cut toilet-paper rolls.

6 Select-a-Shape II—Design a Cylindrical Bone

Did you know?
Your bones are stronger than steel for their weight.

You will need
1 index card (4 x 6 inches)

Ruler

Pencil

Scotch tape

Lightweight paperback books—the same ones in the same order as in activity # 5, Select-a-Shape I, page 56

Your results from activity #5, Select-a-Shape I, page 56.

What do you think?
If I make a cylinder shape out of an index card, it (will) or (won't) be strong enough to hold four lightweight paperback books.

Now you are ready to
1. Draw a line ½ inch in from the 4-inch edge of the index card, using the the ruler and pencil.
2. Roll the index card into a cylinder shape, up to the penciled line. Be sure the half-inch tab is on the outside of the cylinder. Tape the cylinder securely closed.
3. Stand the cylinder on one end and place paperback book #1 on the other end, adding books #2, #3, and so on until the shape can no longer hold the books. Count the number of books the cylinder held. Write the number on the same paper you used to record your results with the rectangle shape.
4. Which shape held more books? How many books could each shape hold?

Brain exercise
The cylinder shape was . . .

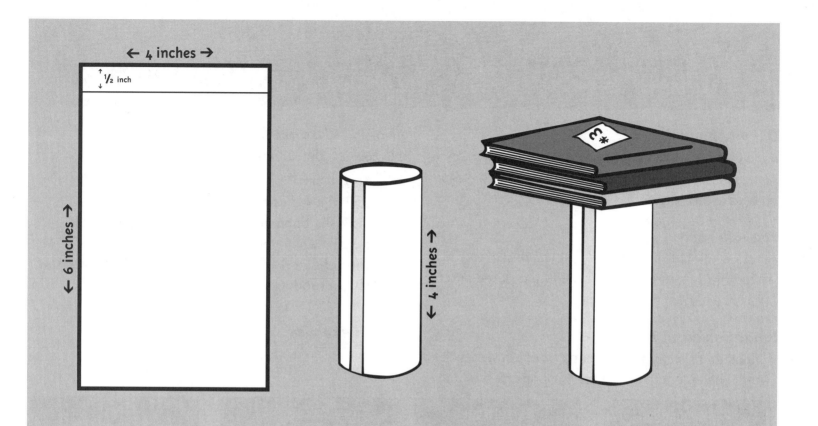

← 4 inches →

↑
½ inch
↓

← 6 inches →

← 4 inches →

<table>
<tr><th>Activity Goal</th><th>Body Note</th><th>Key to Success</th><th>Hint</th></tr>
<tr><td>To test different shapes for strength.</td><td>Your bones are a cylinder-like shape that makes them very strong.</td><td>Use the same lightweight paperback books in the same order for this activity as for activity #5, Select-a-Shape I, on page 56.</td><td>If index cards aren't available, substitute cut toilet-paper rolls.</td></tr>
</table>

Bone Detectives I—Where's the Marrow?

Did you know?

Bone marrow is a jellylike substance found in many of your bones. Bone marrow makes blood cells to keep your body healthy.

You will need

1 cross-sectional slice of cow's femur, rinsed and placed inside a resealable plastic bag (ask the butcher for a slice of beef marrowbone)

What do you think?

If I look at a slice of marrowbone from a cow, I (will) or (won't) be able to feel and see the bone marrow.

Now you are ready to

1. Look at the cut leg bone.

2. Can you see the red center section of the bone?

3. Touch the red center section through the bag. This is the bone marrow. How does it feel? What happens when you touch this part of the bone? The drops of blood you see come from the bone marrow. Marrow produces blood cells.

Brain exercise

When I touched the marrow, it felt . . .

Activity Goal	Body Note	Key to Success	Hint
To see and touch actual bone marrow in a cross section of bone.	Bone marrow manufactures blood cells and stores fat.	Rinse the bone thoroughly, dry it with a paper towel, and then place it in a resealable plastic bag. For health reasons, do not let children touch inside the bag.	Most grocery-store butchers are glad to donate a cut cow femur (marrowbone) for educational purposes. Use the handheld 30X microscope described on page 137 to get a closer look at marrow, or use a magnifying glass.

Did you know?

The outside of your bones (the compact bone) is the second-hardest material in your body.

You will need

Rinsed cow femur in resealable bag from activity #7, Bone Detectives I, page 60
Toothpick

What do you think?

If I look at a cow's leg bone, I (will) or (won't) be able to feel the strength of its compact bone.

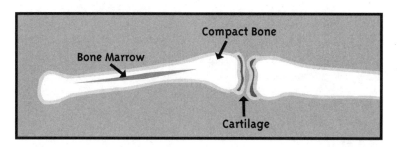

Bone Marrow
Compact Bone
Cartilage

Now you are ready to

1. Look at the cut leg bone through the resealable bag.
2. Can you see the white outer section of the bone?
3. Touch the white outer section through the bag. This is the compact bone. How does it feel? What happens when you touch this part of the bone? Is it hard or soft?
4. Try denting the compact bone with a toothpick. Did it dent the bone?
5. Why do you think bone needs to be so strong?

Brain exercise

When I touched the compact bone, it . . .

Activity Goal	Body Note	Key to Success	Hint
To see and touch compact bone.	Only the enamel on our teeth is harder than compact bone.	Rinse and dry the bone sample after activity #7, Bone Detectives I, on page 60.	You can use the same bone as in activity #7, or you can ask the butcher for a second cut bone. To get another perspective on bone, scoop the marrow out, clean the bone, and let it dry. Use a magnifying glass or a 30X hand-held microscope to view the compact bone more closely.

⑨ See Through! X-Ray Eyes

Did you know?

X rays allow us to see through our skin right to the bones in our skeleton.

You will need

X rays of a foot and an ankle (from a local physician's office)

Light box used by artists, or other bright light source

What do you think?

If I look at an X ray of a foot or ankle, I (will) or (won't) be able to see the individual bones.

Now you are ready to

1. Place each X ray on the light box, one at a time.
2. Can you see the bones on the X rays? Can you count the bones in each X ray?
3. Are you looking at the side of the foot and ankle, or down at the foot?
4. Are the X rays the same or different?

Brain exercise

When I saw the X rays, I thought . . .

Activity Goal	Body Note	Key to Success	Hint
To view X rays of a foot and an ankle. 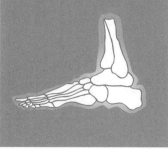	X rays help us to know if our bones are healthy or broken.	The X rays need to be in front of a light source for children to see the details. A small light box works very well.	Many physicians are glad to take and donate non-medical X rays of your feet for educational purposes. If one of your children breaks a bone, ask for permission to share the X rays with the other children. They are fascinated with the X rays.

10 Build a Solid Backbone

Did you know?
Your backbone is made up of 26 small bones. They are called vertebrae.

You will need
1 durable shoelace (as for a workboot)

13 doggy TBonz (from a pet supply store, or see product information, page 137)

Glue or rubber cement

Large resealable plastic bag

What do you think?
If I make a backbone out of many little bones glued together, it (will) or (won't) be very flexible.

Now you are ready to
1. Use the shoelace end to push out the small center section of 13 TBonz.
2. Glue the TBonz together with the glue or rubber cement.
3. Thread the shoelace through the hollow center section of all the TBonz. Tie a knot at both ends.
4. Holding the two ends of the shoelace, try to twist and turn the TBonz into different positions. Is this backbone flexible? Would you want your backbone to act like this?
5. Store the solid backbone inside the resealable bag (the TBonz have a distinct odor).

Brain exercise
If bones can't move, . . .

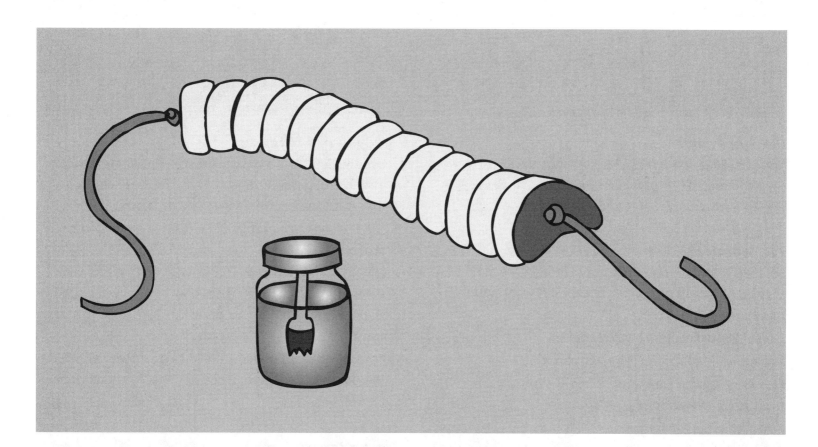

Activity Goal

To observe the limitations of an inflexible backbone.

Body Note

Our backbones need flexibility to twist, turn, bend, and stretch.

Key to Success

Explain that the shoelace is like our spinal cord, and the TBonz are like our vertebrae.

Hint

Discuss ways to build a backbone so that it will be more flexible. Save any leftover materials to use in activity #11, Build a Flexible Backbone, page 66.

⑪ Build a Flexible Backbone

Did you know?

The vertebrae in your backbone are separated by discs of cartilage that fit between the bones. This makes it possible for you to bend and twist.

You will need

Sculpey III modeling compound (look in the clay section of a craft store, or see product information, page 137)

1 sheet (8 inches long) waxed paper

1 durable shoelace (as for a workboot)

13 doggy TBonz (from a pet supply store, or see product information, page 137)

Resealable plastic bag

What do you think?

If I make a backbone with many little bones and discs, it (will) or (won't) be very flexible.

Now you are ready to

1. Use the Sculpey to make 12 discs (flat circles) about an inch in diameter and ⅛-inch thick. Place each disc in its own spot on the waxed paper.

2. Use the shoelace end to push out the small center section of 13 TBonz.

3. Thread the shoelace through 1 TBonz, then through the center of 1 Sculpey disc. Continue to weave the shoelace, alternating bones and discs, until it is woven through all the pieces.

4. Holding the two ends of the shoelace, twist and turn the bones into different positions. Is this backbone flexible?

Brain exercise

When all of the bones could move, the backbone was . . .

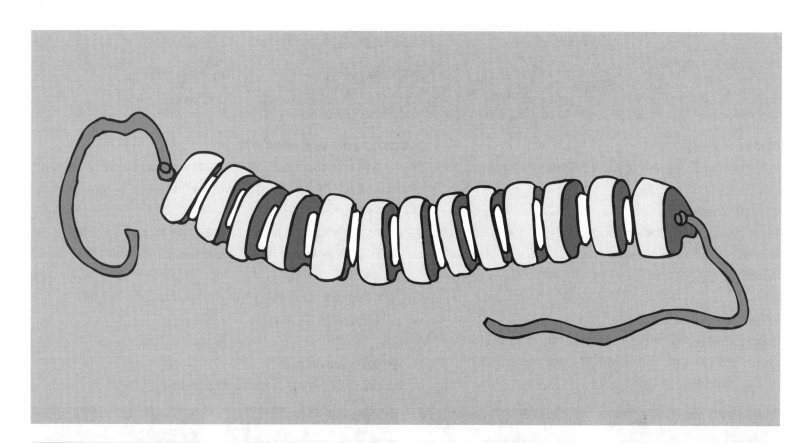

Activity Goal

To create a flexible backbone.

Body Note

Our backbones have flexibility because all of the bones are separate and are cushioned by the discs. This backbone also protects our spinal column.

Key to Success

Explain that the shoelace is like our spinal cord, the Sculpey is like our discs, and the TBonz are like our vertebrae.

Hint

Make the discs large enough that they don't fall apart. Center the holes in the discs so that they stay on the shoelace. Store the flexible backbone in the resealable bag.

Did you know?

Your height changes as you go through your day.

You will need

Tape measure or Our Height Bar Graph, page 32
Paper
Pencil

What do you think?

If I am measured in the morning, my height will be the (same as) or (different than) if I get measured in the late afternoon or night.

Now you are ready to

1. Ask a friend or adult to measure you as early as you can in the morning. Record your early height on the paper.

2. Ask a friend or adult to measure you as late in the day as you can. Record your late height on the paper.

3. Compare your early height to your late height. Is there any difference?

Brain exercise

When I was measured the second time, I was . . .

Activity Goal	Body Note	Key to Success	Hint
To see how height changes during the day.	The cartilage discs between the vertebrae in our backbones swell as they collect fluid during the night. This makes us taller in the morning. Standing during the day squeezes some of the fluid out, which makes us shorter in the evening.	Taking accurate measurements is very important to the success of this activity.	Separate the measurement times as much as possible for the most dramatic changes in height.

Match Up! Where's That Bone?

Did you know?
Your bones give your body its shape.

You will need
Where's That Bone? Bingo Board, page 70, copied onto white card stock

Where's That Bone? Picture Cards, page 71, copied onto white card stock

Scissors

Answer sheet, page 136

Now you are ready to
1. Cut out all of the picture cards.
2. Look at your Where's That Bone? Bingo Board.

Find the picture card that you think goes with each number on the board.

3. Check the answer sheet on page 136 to see how many numbers you matched.
4. Did you make a bingo?
5. Try playing bingo again later and see how much you've learned.

Brain exercise
When I first played Where's That Bone? Bingo, I . . .

Activity Goal	Body Note	Key to Success	Hint
To identify bones from different places in the body.	The skull has many bones that have grown together.	Read and discuss the information in My Body at Work, page 45, before the children play this bingo game.	Children love learning about their bones. Bingo is a fun way for them to learn what their bones actually look like.

Where's That Bone? Bingo Board

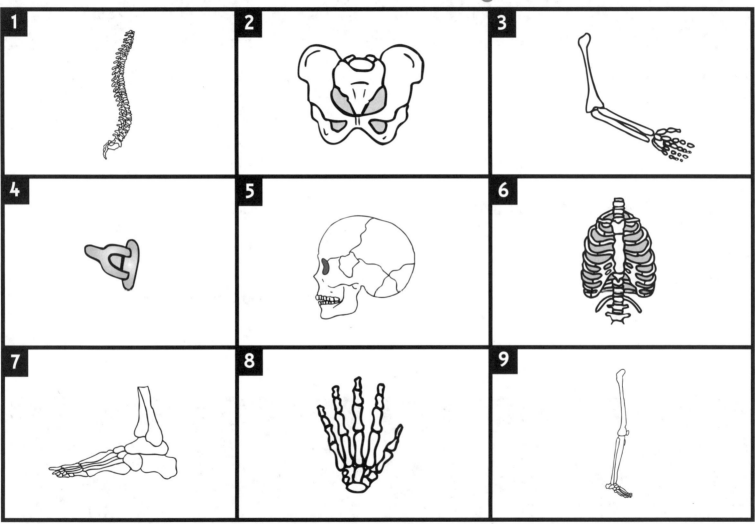

Where's That Bone? Picture Cards

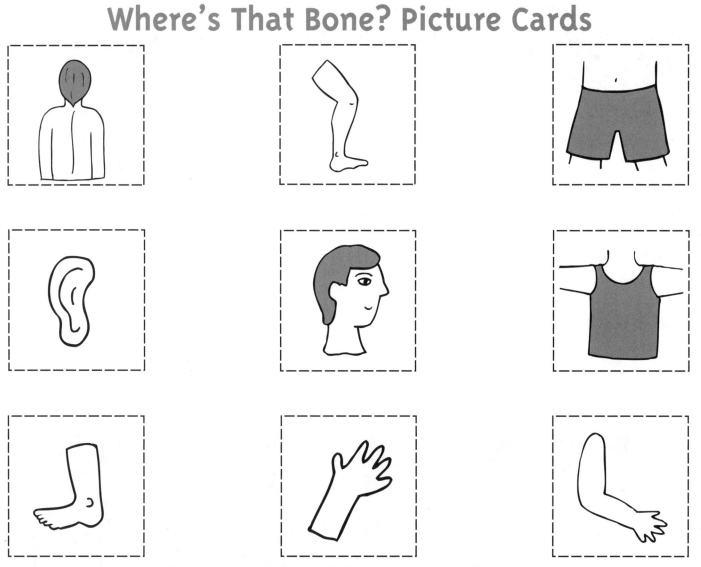

Did you know?

Your feet and hands house more than half the bones in your body.

You will need

Name That Number! Bingo Board, page 73, copied onto yellow card stock

Name That Number! cards, page 74, copied onto yellow card stock

Scissors

Answer sheet, page 136

Now you are ready to

1. Cut out all the Name That Number! cards.
2. Look at your Name That Number! Bingo Board. Find the picture that you think goes with each number card.
3. Check the answer sheet, page 136, to see how many numbers you matched.
4. Did you make a bingo?
5. Try playing bingo again later and see how much you've learned.

Brain exercise

When I first played Name That Number!, I . . .

Activity Goal	Body Note	Key to Success	Hint
To learn how many bones are in different places in the body.	Besides giving your body shape, your bones work with your muscles to help you move and to protect your organs.	Read and discuss the information in *My Body at Work*, page 45, before the children play this bingo game.	Children really enjoy making a best guess on the bone numbers. Eventually, they will know them all.

Name That Number! Bingo Board

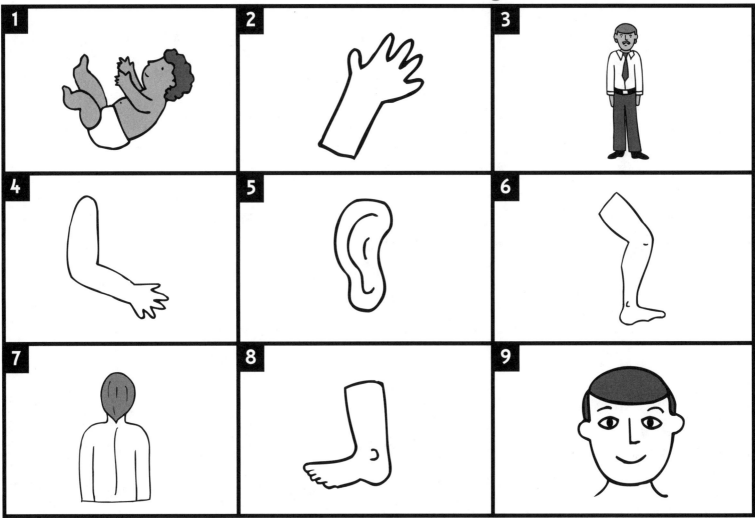

Name That Number! Cards

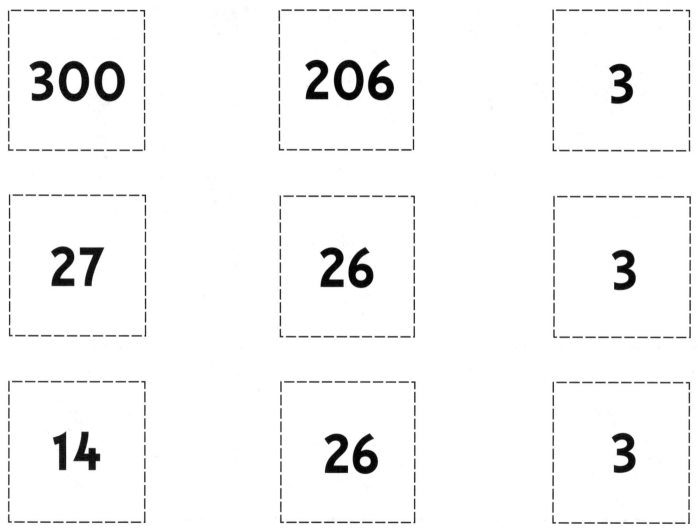

300	206	3
27	26	3
14	26	3

15 Measure That Bone!

Did you know?
If you are eating properly and exercising, your bones will continue to grow until you are about 18 years old.

You will need
Cloth measuring tape (found in fabric stores)
My Bones Grow! sheet, page 76
Partner
"All About Me" Growth Portfolio Notebook, page 39
Hole punch

What do you think?
If my partner measures from the top of my shoulder to my elbow, I predict that the measurement will be more than _____ inches.

Now you are ready to
1. Ask your partner to measure from the top of your shoulder to the bottom of your elbow.
2. Write the number of inches on the My Bones Grow! sheet, page 76.
3. Measure your leg from the front of your ankle to the front of your knee.
4. Record the length of this bone on the My Bones Grow! sheet.
5. Hole-punch your My Bones Grow! sheet and place it in your growth portfolio.
6. Measure again in 3 months to see how you have grown.

Brain exercise
When I measured my leg, I . . .

My Bones Grow! Sheet

Date	Leg bone measurement	Arm bone measurement
_____	_____	_____
_____	_____	_____
_____	_____	_____
_____	_____	_____
_____	_____	_____
_____	_____	_____
_____	_____	_____
_____	_____	_____

Watch Me Grow, © 1999. Published by Chicago Review Press, Inc., 800-888-7471.

Activity Goal

To practice measuring and recording bone growth.

Body Note

You will be measuring your humerus (upper arm bone) and your fibula or tibia (lower leg bones).

Key to Success

Model how to measure the upper arm bone and the lower leg bone.

Hint

Use soft cloth measuring tapes. They are very inexpensive. Children enjoy having a measuring tape of their own and take great delight in measuring everything in sight.

Mighty Muscles

Mighty Muscles

Mighty muscles wiggle my toes,
Mighty muscles crinkle my nose,
Mighty muscles put on my clothes.
I really use my muscles!

Working together, two by two,
Contract and relax is what they do,
Pulling the weight for me and you.
I really use my muscles!

Mighty muscles move my feet,
Mighty muscles chew my treat,
Mighty muscles snap the beat,
I really use my muscles!

Sung to "Lou, Lou, Skip to My Lou"

In Mighty Muscles you will find

Wonderful Words About My Mighty Muscles

Contracting Muscles

Your muscles contract to pull on your bones and make your body move. As muscles contract, they get shorter and thicker.

Involuntary Muscles

Muscles that work automatically, like your heart muscle, are called involuntary muscles. You don't have to think about these muscles to make them work.

Muscle Fibers

Muscle fibers are the long skinny cells that make up your muscles.

Reflex

Your reflexes are automatic reactions to something. Reflexes are so fast that you don't even have time to think about them. Reflexes protect you from danger.

Relaxing Muscles

Your muscles relax by becoming longer and thinner. Muscles naturally move to their relaxed state to conserve energy.

Voluntary Muscles

The muscles that you have control over, like the muscles in your fingers, toes, legs, and arms, are called voluntary muscles.

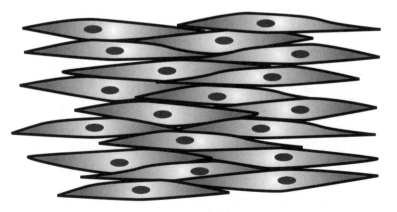

Muscle Fibers

My Body at Work

What should I know about my mighty muscles?

✪ Your body has over 600 muscles. They help you to wiggle your ears, scratch your nose, stand up straight, and curl your toes. These actions require hundreds of your muscles working together.

✪ Muscles get their energy from your blood supply. Muscles use up a lot of energy. Your blood supply provides them with oxygen from the air you breathe and nutrients from the food that you eat.

✪ Muscles move bones by contracting. This means they get shorter and thicker. They move according to the instructions given by your brain.

✪ Muscles can't push, they can only pull. This is why many muscles work in pairs, as when one muscle bends your elbow and then the other straightens it.

✪ Your muscles are made up of thousands of long skinny cells called muscle fibers. Some muscle fibers are thinner than one strand of your hair. Each fiber can only contract for a fraction of a second at a time.

✪ Voluntary muscles are those muscles that you can control, like your fingers, toes, legs, and arms, by just thinking about them.

✪ Involuntary muscles are muscles like those in your heart and stomach. You don't have to think about them to make them move. There are certain muscles that are both voluntary and involuntary, like the muscles used in blinking.

✪ Exercise makes your muscles stronger and larger. It is very important to exercise your muscles so that they won't get weaker and smaller.

My Mighty Muscles Journal

Today I learned

Watch Me Grow, © 1999. Published by Chicago Review Press, Inc., 800-888-7471.

1 Best Guess—Muscle Trivia Cards

Did you know?
You have over 600 muscles in your body.

You will need
2 sheets (8½ x 11 inches) colored card stock

Muscle Trivia card fronts, page 85, copied onto one sheet of card stock

Muscle Trivia card backs, page 86, copied onto other sheet of card stock

Scissors

Glue

Partner (one partner needs to be able to read)

Rubber band

What do you think?
If I try to guess the answers for the muscle trivia questions, I predict that I will guess _____ out of 4 correctly.

Now you are ready to
1. Cut out the 16 Muscle Trivia cards from both sheets of card stock.

2. Match the question fronts to their answer backs. Glue the matching card pieces together, back to back. Laminate if you like.

3. Place the cards with the question side up.

4. Ask your partner to give a best guess answer to the first four questions. If one of you can't read, the partner who can read should read each question aloud. Once a question is answered, check the back of the card to see if it was answered correctly. How well did your partner guess?

5. Next, it is your turn to guess the answers to questions 5–8. How well did you guess?

6. Try answering the questions again. See how many you can get right this time. Over time you'll be surprised at how much you know about your muscles. Place the rubber band around the cards to save them for future use.

Brain exercise
When I guessed the answers, I . . .

Activity Goal	Key to Success	Hint
To learn new information about muscles in a fun trivia card game.	One partner needs to be able to read. Children may need help with cutting out the cards.	Place the cards in an activity center for children to play with whenever they have free time.

Muscle Trivia Card Fronts

Muscle Trivia ①	Muscle Trivia ②	Muscle Trivia ③	Muscle Trivia ④
What is our largest muscle?	What is our smallest muscle?	What is our stongest muscle?	What is our longest muscle?

Muscle Trivia ⑤	Muscle Trivia ⑥	Muscle Trivia ⑦	Muscle Trivia ⑧
How many muscles are in your body?	How many muscles are in your face?	What uses more muscles? 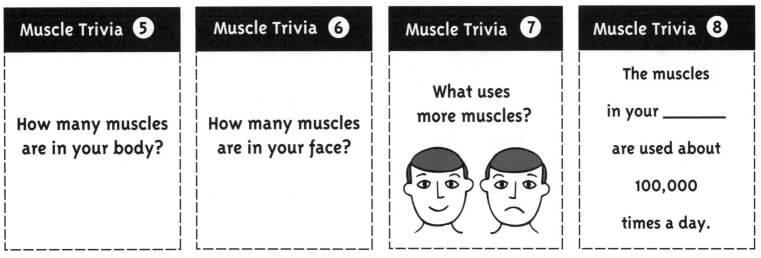	The muscles in your _____ are used about 100,000 times a day.

Watch Me Grow, © 1999. Published by Chicago Review Press, Inc., 800-888-7471.

Muscle Trivia Card Backs

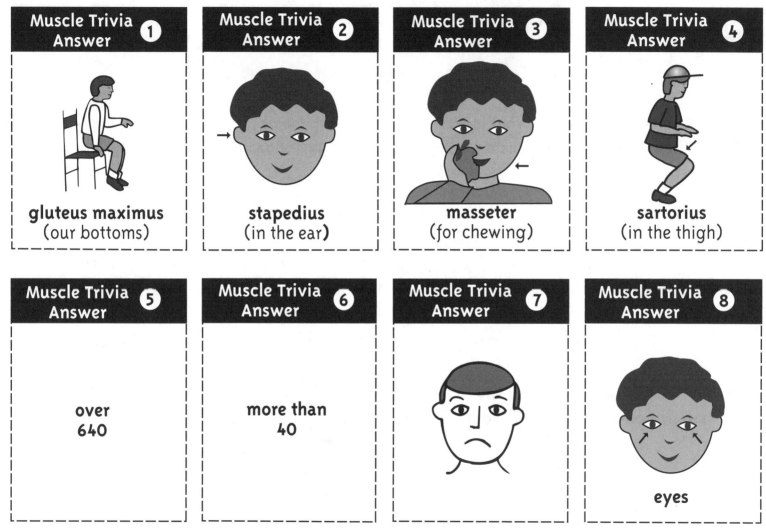

Muscle Trivia Answer 1

gluteus maximus
(our bottoms)

Muscle Trivia Answer 2

stapedius
(in the ear)

Muscle Trivia Answer 3

masseter
(for chewing)

Muscle Trivia Answer 4

sartorius
(in the thigh)

Muscle Trivia Answer 5

over
640

Muscle Trivia Answer 6

more than
40

Muscle Trivia Answer 7

Muscle Trivia Answer 8

eyes

Watch Me Grow, © 1999. Published by Chicago Review Press, Inc., 800-888-7471.

② Magnify a Muscle

Did you know?
Your muscles are made up of long skinny cells called muscle fibers. Some muscle fibers are thinner than one strand of your hair.

You will need
Very thin slice of steak (ask your local butcher)

2 glass slides or a slide with a slide cover

Tweezers

Plastic needle

1 drop blue food coloring

1 drop red food coloring

Rubbing alcohol (about 1 teaspoonful)

Small container with lid

Eyedropper

Magnifying glass and/or 30X handheld microscope (see product information, page 137)

Soap and water for cleanup

What do you think?
If I put a thin slice of steak in between two microscope slides, I (will) or (won't) be able to see muscle fibers.

Now you are ready to
1. Pick up the thin slice of steak with the tweezers and place it in the middle of a slide.
2. Use the plastic needle to separate the muscle fibers.
3. Make a food-color stain by combining the blue and red food color with the rubbing alcohol in a small container. Place the lid on top and shake the mixture.
4. Use the eye dropper to place a drop of stain on top of the steak resting on the slide.
5. Place the other slide over the top of the stained steak.
6. Use your magnifying glass or microscope to look at the individual muscle fibers.

Brain exercise
When I looked at the muscle, I thought . . .

Activity Goal

To see muscle fibers.

Body Note

A whole muscle consists of bundles of muscle fibers.

Key to Success

Make sure the muscle fibers have been teased apart and the magnifying glass is strong enough to magnify the muscle to show the fibers.

Hint

For a wonderful portable, handheld 30X microscope, look at the inexpensive microscope produced by Tasco (see product information, page 137, for details).

Model a Muscle—Finger Play

Did you know?

Your muscles can either contract or relax. When a muscle is contracted, it is shorter and thicker in the middle. When a muscle is relaxed, it is longer and thinner in the middle.

You will need

You

Both hands

Desk

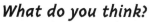

What do you think?

If I lace my fingers together, they (will) or (won't) look like a contracting muscle.

Now you are ready to

1. Place your hands on a desk with the fingers of each hand pointing toward each other.

2. Slide your hands together so that three fingers (not the baby finger) are barely laced together. Your hands are now like a muscle in a relaxing position. Do they lie flat or are they bunched up?

3. Continue to slide your fingers together until they can't slide any further. Together, your hands are now like a muscle in a contracting position. Do they lie flat or are they bunched up?

Brain exercise

When I laced my fingers together, they were like . . .

Activity Goal	Body Note	Key to Success	Hint
To model the way a muscle looks contracting and relaxing.	Each of your muscle fibers contain thin rods that slide past each other as your fingers did to make the muscle fiber contract (shorten).	Hands need to be flat on the table to start this activity.	This activity should be done before activity #7, Bodybuilder Muscles, page 94.

Did you know?

Many muscles are hard at work even when you are sleeping.

You will need

Timer
You
Partner

What do you think?

If I tell my muscles to stay still for 30 seconds, I (will) or (won't) be able to stop all of my muscles from moving.

Now you are ready to

1. Set the timer for 30 seconds.
2. Sit cross-legged on the floor. Tell your muscles to stop moving. Try to sit still until the timer goes off.
3. Ask your partner to watch you as you try to sit still.
4. Do you think you were able to stop moving?
What happened? How hard was it to stay still? What muscles moved even when you tried to stay perfectly still?
5. Did your partner think that you moved?

Brain exercise

When I tried to stop moving, my muscles . . .

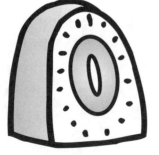

Activity Goal

To explore the concept of involuntary muscles.

Body Note

When we sit still or sleep, we still have many muscles working in our bodies. We don't have to tell them what to do. They are called involuntary muscles. They work without our controlling them. Our heart muscle pumps blood and never rests. Our eyes blink automatically about every four seconds and our chests move up and down so that we can breathe.

Key to Success

It is important to have your partner observe your movement and report back to you.

Hint

Discuss things we can control with our muscles and the things our muscles do automatically.

Did you know?

Reflexes happen automatically. We don't have to think about them.

You will need

You

Partner

Chair (high enough that a seated child's feet do not touch the floor)

What do you think?

If I gently hit my partner's leg just below the knee, my partner's leg (will) or (won't) fly up automatically.

Now you are ready to

1. Ask your partner to sit on the edge of a chair so that his or her feet don't touch the floor.

2. Standing to the side of your partner, gently hit your partner's leg just below his or her knee with the side of your flat hand.

3. What happened? If nothing happened, you might not have found the right spot. Keep trying until something happens.

Brain exercise

When I saw my partner's leg fly up, I thought . . .

Activity Goal	Body Note	Key to Success	Hint
To see a reflex in action.	Doctors test reflexes to check the nervous system.	Have children stand to the side so they won't accidentally be kicked.	Show children how to do this activity before they try it.

6 Muscle Music? Dancing Twists

Did you know?

Muscles are made of thousands of cells called muscle fibers. Each fiber can only contract for a fraction of a second at a time.

You will need

You

Tie twist (as for a large plastic trash bag)

Metal ruler

Desk

What do you think?

If I hold a metal ruler with a tie twist hanging over it, I (will) or (won't) be able to keep the twist from dancing.

Now you are ready to

1. Bend the twist over the ruler so that it hangs evenly.
2. Using one arm only (no other support), hold the twist as close to the desk as possible without letting it move.
3. What happened to the twist? Could you keep it from dancing? Why do you think this happened?

Brain exercise

When I held the hanging twist close to the desk, . . .

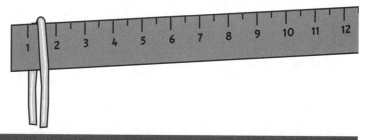

Activity Goal	Body Note	Key to Success	Hint
To see your own muscle contractions.	After a few seconds, the twist started moving to the beat of your muscle contractions.	Children need to keep the tie twist as close to the desk as possible .	The arm holding the ruler must be unsupported.

7 Bodybuilder Muscles

Did you know?
Two main muscles help you to lower and raise your hands. They are called your triceps and your biceps.

You will need
You
Your arm

What do you think?
If I lift my hand I (will) or (won't) be able to tell which muscle is contracting.

Now you are ready to
1. Hold your right arm down at your side. Place your left hand on your bodybuilder muscle (biceps), which is in the front part of your upper arm.
2. Feel your biceps muscle as you lift your right hand. Could you feel the muscle get bigger and shorter? Your biceps muscle pulls (contracts) to lift up your hand.

3. Keep your hand up. Feel your biceps muscle relax as you lower your right hand. Did you feel your biceps muscle get smaller and longer? Now it is relaxed.
4. Put your hand up again. This time feel the back part of your upper arm when you lower your right hand. This is your triceps muscle. It pulls (contracts) to straighten out your elbow and lower your hand.

Brain exercise
When I raised my hand, my biceps muscles . . .

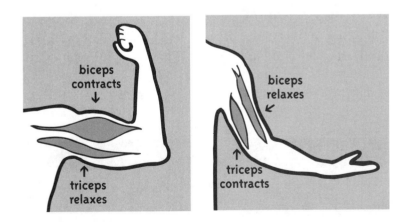

biceps contracts

↓

triceps relaxes

↑

biceps relaxes

↙

triceps contracts

↑

Activity Goal	Body Note	Key to Success	Hint
To learn about how muscles work in pairs.	The full names for these muscles are the biceps brachii and the triceps brachii.	Check to see that children have identified the correct muscle.	Another way to see these muscles in action is to take turns placing one hand palm up under the edge of a desk and gently lifting the desk up (use moderate pressure— do not strain) with a partner feeling both muscles.

8 Totally Tired Muscles

Did you know?
All muscles get tired after exercising.

You will need
Timer
Left hand

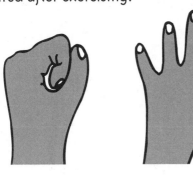

What do you think?
If I open and close my left hand once a second, it (will) or (won't) get tired in 2 minutes.

Now you are ready to
1. Set the timer for 2 minutes.
2. Open and close the fingers on your left hand once a second for the next 2 minutes if you can.
3. Stop if your hand gets too tired.
4. If your hand didn't get too tired in 2 minutes, see how long it takes before you need to stop.
5. What did it feel like when your hand got tired?

Brain exercise
When I tried to exercise my left hand without stopping, it . . .

Activity Goal	Body Note	Key to Success	Hint
To show how muscles tire with exercise.	When muscles get tired, they use up oxygen faster than your body can supply it. This can hurt and cause muscle cramps or muscle tightness.	Continuous exercise is necessary for the muscles to tire.	Children enjoy watching the timer as they exercise.

Did you know?

Your muscles use up a lot of energy when they are exercised.

You will need

Your fingers
Your brain

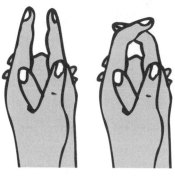

What do you think?

If I relax my pointer fingers while my hands are folded with my pointer fingers standing straight up, I (will) or (won't) be able to keep my pointer fingers standing.

Now you are ready to

1. Fold your hands together.
2. Stand your pointer fingers up straight. Don't let them rest on each other. Keep them standing.
3. Relax your pointer fingers. What happened when you stopped telling your fingers to stand up straight?

Brain exercise

When I relaxed my pointer fingers, they . . .

Activity Goal	Body Note	Key to Success	Hint
To see how muscles relax when they are no longer needed.	In order to conserve energy, your muscles naturally go back to a relaxed position. This is why your fingers moved together in this activity.	In order to demonstrate this concept, pointer fingers need to be independent of each other. They cannot be resting on each other.	Some children may need help placing their hands into the right position.

Practice Makes Perfect

Did you know?

Movements you practice become easier to do and take less and less practice.

You will need

You

Desk

What do you think?

If I tap my right-hand fingers on a desk with my fingertips facing down, it (will) or (won't) be easier than tapping with my fingertips facing up.

Now you are ready to

1. Tap the desk with your fingertips facing down. Tap in a row (pointer, middle finger, ring finger, baby finger). Is this something you do very often? Was it very hard for you to do?

2. Turn your hand over on the desk. Tap the desk with your fingertips facing up. Tap in a row (pointer, middle finger, ring finger, baby finger). Is this something you do very often? Was it very hard for you to do? Was it harder or easier than tapping with your fingertips up?

3. Practice tapping this new way for a week. Did it change your performance?

Brain exercise

When I tapped with my fingers facing up, it was . . .

Activity Goal	Body Note	Key to Success	Hint
To see how practice influences muscle performance.	Muscles learn with repetition. The muscles used for tapping with your fingertips facing down have been used more often, so they are stronger and more coordinated than muscles used for tapping with your fingertips up.	Discuss with the children how muscles improve with practice like the muscles we use when we catch a ball or ride a bike or play the piano.	If children have difficulty tapping with fingertips up, demonstrate it for them.

11 Talented Muscles—Power or Precision?

Did you know?
Your wrists and hands have more than 30 muscles.

You will need
Adult
Plastic needle with large eye
1 piece (6 inches) thin ribbon
Hackysack

Now you are ready to
1. Take the plastic needle in your left hand and thread the piece of ribbon through the needle. You were using your muscles of precision.

2. Ask an adult to hold the plastic needle between his or her thumb and first finger. This is called a precision grip.

3. Grab the hackysack and clench it in your fist. Throw the hackysack up in the air and catch it. You are using your muscles of power. When you clenched the hackysack, you were using a power grip. It used very different muscles than the precision grip.

Brain exercise
When I threaded the needle, my muscles . . .

Activity Goal	Body Note	Key to Success	Hint
To identify two very different muscle functions.	Your muscles make it possible for you to perform very precise movements like holding a paintbrush, cutting with scissors, and threading a needle. They also give you the ability to use force when gripping bicycle handlebars or opening a door.	Show children how to thread a needle before they attempt to do it.	Plastic needles need to have large eyes for threading and blunt ends.

Did you know?

If certain movements are repeated, your muscles adjust and become accustomed to them.

You will need

You

Partner

Clock with
second hand

What do you think?

If pressure is exerted on my arm as I try to lift it up, it (will) or (won't) stay down when I stop lifting up and the pressure is taken off.

Now you are ready to

1. Select a partner to do this activity with you. Ask your partner to stand next to you and hold your right hand straight down by your side. Your partner needs to push carefully so you won't be hurt.

2. Try to lift your arm up in a straight position as your partner carefully pushes down on it.

3. After 20 to 30 seconds stop lifting and ask your partner to let go of your arm.

4. What happened to your arm? Did your arm rise up? Why do you think this happened?

5. Switch places with your partner, and repeat steps 1–3. Does the same thing happen to your partner?

Brain exercise

When my partner let go of my arm, it . . .

Activity Goal	Body Note	Key to Success	Hint
To show how muscles adjust to a new situation.	When your partner let go of your arm, it took a few seconds for your muscles to adjust to the new situation.	Arms need to be straight down at the siides.	Demonstrate this activity by playing the role of partner with a child.

Trick a Muscle II—Double the Fun?

Did you know?

You can do two things at once—it just takes practice. Practice makes this trick easier.

You will need

You

Partner

What do you think?

If I rub my stomach, I (will) or (won't) be able to pat my head at the same time.

Now you are ready to

1. Choose a partner. Ask your partner to watch you as you try to master this muscle activity.

2. Rub your left hand in circles on your stomach. Were you able to do that? Was it easy or hard to do?

3. Pat your head with your right hand. Were you able to do that? Was it easy or hard to do?

4. Now pat your head with your right hand as you rub your stomach with your left hand. Were you able to do that? Was it easy or hard to do?

5. Ask your partner to watch you as you practice doing this. Does your partner think you are getting better at it?

6. Observe as your partner follows steps 2–4.

Brain exercise

When I tried to do two things at once, . . .

Activity Goal	Body Note	Key to Success	Hint
To experience the difficulty of using two muscle sets at once.	Repetition improves our muscle coordination.	Allow children the opportunity to master each skill before combining the skills.	Practice this skill over time to show how muscles learn and adjust.

Did you know?

No matter where you travel, people around the world can recognize at least five of your feelings by the expression on your face.

You will need

You

Partner

What do you think?

If I pretend I am sad, my partner (will) or (won't) know it.

Now you are ready to

1. Choose a partner. Ask your partner to name your feeling when you make a face.

2. Pretend that you are sad. Did your partner say the feeling was sad?

3. Pretend that you are happy. Was your partner correct?

4. Pretend that you are mad. Could your partner identify the feeling?

5. Pretend that you are afraid. Did your partner correctly name what you were feeling?

6. Pretend that you are surprised. Was this easy for your partner to identify?

7. How many times was your partner correct in guessing your feeling?

8. See if you can tell what your partner is feeling through his or her facial expressions.

Brain exercise

When my partner smiled, I knew . . .

Activity Goal	Body Note	Key to Success	Hint
To see the muscles of expression at work.	You use more than 40 muscles in expressing all of your different feelings.	Children need to feel comfortable making faces.	If you are working with a large group, ask children to volunteer as a model for each feeling.

15 Measure That Muscle!

Did you know?
If you are eating properly and exercising, your muscles will grow stronger and larger.

You will need
Partner

Cloth measuring tape (found in fabric store}

My Muscles Grow! sheet, page 104, copied onto white paper

"All About Me" Growth Portfolio Notebook, page 39

Hole punch

What do you think?
If my partner measures my right biceps muscle, I predict that it will be more than _____ inches.

Now you are ready to
1. Ask your partner to measure the bodybuilder muscle on your right arm.
2. Write the number of inches measured on the My Muscles Grow! sheet, page 104.
3. Measure your calf muscles (around the widest section of the calf) on your right leg.
4. Write the number of inches down on the My Muscles Grow! sheet, page 104.
5. Hole-punch your muscle sheet and place it in your growth portfolio.
6. Measure again in 3 months to see how you have grown.

Brain exercise
When I measured my calf muscles, I . . .

Activity Goal	Body Note	Key to Success	Hint
To practice measurement and record muscle growth.	You will be measuring your biceps muscle in your upper arm and your tibalis and gastrocnemius muscles in your calf.	Model how to measure the upper arm muscle and the calf muscles.	Use soft cloth measuring tapes. They are very inexpensive. Children enjoy having a measuring tape of their own and take great delight in measuring everything in sight.

My Muscles Grow! Sheet

Date	Arm muscle measurement	Calf muscle measurement
_____	_____	_____
_____	_____	_____
_____	_____	_____
_____	_____	_____
_____	_____	_____
_____	_____	_____
_____	_____	_____

Watch Me Grow, © 1999. Published by Chicago Review Press, Inc., 800-888-7471.

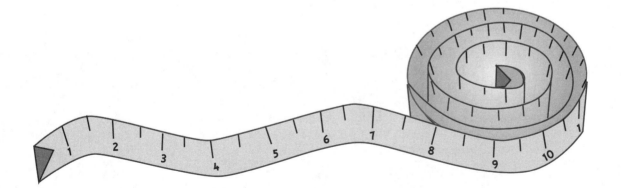

Connections

My Connections

Bone to muscle, bone to bone,
My connections hold their own.

Joints are where bones move and meet.
Gliding joints are in my feet.

Bone to muscle, bone to bone,
My connections hold their own.

Ropelike tendons tough and strong
Bind bone to muscle all day long.

Bone to muscle, bone to bone,
My connections hold their own.

Straplike ligaments hold and stretch
Bones to bones they're meant to catch.

Bone to muscle, bone to bone,
My connections hold their own.

Sung to "Twinkle, Twinkle, Little Star"

In Connections you will find

Wonderful Words About My Connections

Ball-and-Socket Joint Your ball-and-socket joints are the most flexible joints in your body. They allow your arms to move up and down, backward, forward, and all around.

Cartilage Cartilage is a rubbery substance found at the tip of your nose, on the tops of your ears, the tips of your bones, and in between the vertebrae in your back.

Fixed Joint Most joints are flexible, but some are fixed so that they don't move. The bones in your skull grow together and become fixed joints.

Gliding Joint Your gliding joints allow your bones to glide and slide across each other to a limited extent in a number of directions. Your toes and fingers have gliding joints.

Hinge Joint Your hinge joints open and close like a door. You have more hinge joints than any other type of joint. They allow your elbows to bend.

Humerus bone The humerus bone is sometimes called your "funny bone." It is the bone found in your upper arm.

Joint A joint is a place in your body where two or more bones meet. Some of your joints are movable and some are fixed.

Ligament A ligament is a band of somewhat elastic tissue that connects your bones to each other.

Pivot Joint A pivot joint is found in only two places in your body. It allows your wrists and your neck to rotate.

Saddle Joint Your saddle joint is a very important joint found only in your thumb. In this joint, your bone ends are shaped like saddles and slide over each other. The saddle joint allows your thumb to tilt in all directions.

Synovial Fluid Synovial fluid is an oil-like substance produced by your body to lubricate and protect your joints.

Tendon A tendon is a band of strong ropelike tissue that connects a muscle to a bone.

My Body at Work

What should I know about my connections?

✪ Your bones are connected by joints, strong straps called ligaments, and muscles. Muscles are attached to bones by strong, ropelike tissues called tendons. You learned about bones and muscles in the second and third chapters of this book.

✪ Ligaments are like strong rubber bands. They hold your bones in place. Some people have very loose ligaments. This makes them seem very flexible, or "double-jointed." Ligaments have some elasticity. This allows your bone movement to be more flexible.

✪ Tendons are very tough, much like strong, tough rope. They securely connect your muscles to your bones. You can see them and feel them through your skin.

✪ Cartilage is the rubbery substance you can feel at the tip of your nose. It is found on the ends of your bones, in between your vertebrae, and in other places in your body that need protection from everyday wear and tear. Many times, cartilage works with an oil-like substance called synovial fluid produced by your body to protect your joints.

✪ Joints are usually found where bones meet and move together. Working with muscles, your joints give your body a wide range of possible movements. They make it possible for you to bend, stretch up toward the sun, swivel your head from side to side, snap, point your fingers, pivot turn, and clench your fist.

✪ Some of your bones are locked together in fixed joints. Others move freely, with cartilage and synovial fluid to protect them.

✪ Your hinge joints open and close like a door. Your ball-and-socket joints are more flexible than any other joints and let your arms move up and down, backward, forward, and all around. The pivot joint in your neck allows your head to rotate from side to side. Your gliding joints make it possible for the bones in your toes and fingers to glide and slide a bit in a number of directions. The saddle joints of your thumbs help you make the very precise movements that are needed in writing and painting.

My Connections Journal

Today I learned

① Best Guess—Connections Trivia Cards

Did you know?

Your bones are held together at joints. Bones are attached to bones at joints. Muscles are attached to bones by strong, ropelike tissue called tendons. You have over 100 joints in your body.

You will need

2 sheets (8½ x 11 inches) card stock

Connections Trivia card fronts, page 113, copied onto one sheet of card stock

Connections Trivia card backs, page 114, copied onto the other sheet of card stock

Scissors

Glue

Partner (one partner needs to be able to read)

Rubber band

What do you think?

If I try to guess the answers for the connections trivia questions, I will guess _____ out of 4 correctly.

Now you are ready to

1. Cut out the 16 Connections Trivia cards from both sheets of card stock.

2. Match the question fronts to their answer backs. Glue the matching card pieces together, back to back. Laminate if you like.

3. Place the cards with the question side up.

4. Ask your partner to give a best-guess answer to the first four questions. If one of you can't read, the partner who can read should read each question aloud. Once a question is answered, check the back of the card to see if it was answered correctly. How well did your partner guess?

5. Next, it is your turn to guess the answers to questions 5–8. How well did you guess?

6. Try answering the questions again. See how many you can get right this time. Over time you'll be surprised at how much you know about your connections. Place the rubber band around the cards to save them for future use.

Brain exercise

When I guessed the answers, I . . .

Activity Goal

To learn new information about your connections in a fun trivia card game.

Key to Success

One partner needs to be able to read. Children may need help with cutting out the cards.

Hint

Use a rubber band or resealable sandwich bag to keep the cards together.

Connections Trivia Card Fronts

Connections Trivia **1**	Connections Trivia **2**	Connections Trivia **3**	Connections Trivia **4**
Where is our largest joint?	Where is our smallest joint?	Where is cartilage found? (4 places in your body)	Fixed joints are found in the . . .

Connections Trivia **5**	Connections Trivia **6**	Connections Trivia **7**	Connections Trivia **8**
What is more slippery than ice?	What connects bone to bone?	What connects muscle to bone?	Loose ligaments cause . . .

Watch Me Grow, © 1999. Published by Chicago Review Press, Inc., 800-888-7471.

Connections Trivia Card Backs

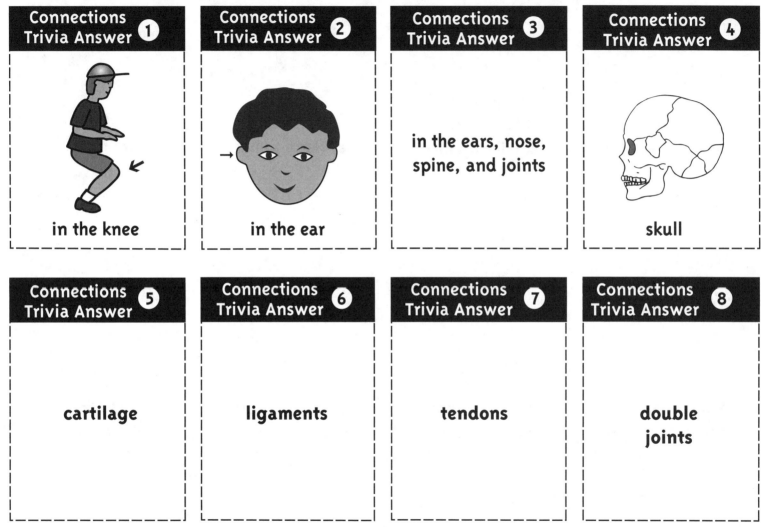

Connections Trivia Answer ①	Connections Trivia Answer ②	Connections Trivia Answer ③	Connections Trivia Answer ④
in the knee	in the ear	in the ears, nose, spine, and joints	skull

Connections Trivia Answer ⑤	Connections Trivia Answer ⑥	Connections Trivia Answer ⑦	Connections Trivia Answer ⑧
cartilage	ligaments	tendons	double joints

Watch Me Grow, © 1999. Published by Chicago Review Press, Inc., 800-888-7471.

2 Cushy Cartilage

Did you know?
The tip of your nose is made out of cartilage. Cartilage is a tough, spongy material.

You will need
- Your ears
- Your nose
- Your head

What do you think?
If I feel my nose, I (will) or (won't) know what cartilage feels like.

Now you are ready to
1. Touch the end of your nose with your pointer finger. How does it feel? Does your finger bounce when you touch it?

2. Carefully push down on the very top section of the outside of your right ear with your right pointer finger. Describe how it feels. Does it feel like the end of your nose?

3. Touch your left pointer finger to your forehead. Does your finger bounce when you touch your forehead? How is your forehead different than your nose?

Brain exercise
When I touched my nose and then my forehead, my forehead . . .

Activity Goal	Body Note	Key to Success	Hint
To learn about cartilage.	Your nose and the outside of your ears have cartilage instead of bone. It feels spongy. The cartilage discs between the vertebrae in your back act like shock absorbers to cushion your bones.	Children need to touch the tips of their noses and the tops of their ears in order to feel the cartilage.	To see the difference between bone and cartilage, ask children to take a partner and watch his or her nose move when touched.

3 Two Tenacious Tendons

Did you know?
Your muscles are attached to bone by strong, narrow, ropelike tissues called tendons. Tendons help your muscles to move bone.

You will need
You
Your inside arm
The back of your knee

What do you think?
If I make a fist with my right hand, I (will) or (won't) be able to feel the tendon connecting my biceps muscle to my arm bones.

Now you are ready to
1. Make a bodybuilder fist with your right hand.
2. Take your left hand and feel the inside part of your elbow.
3. Do you feel the strong attachment from the muscle to your bone? That is the tendon that attaches your biceps to your lower arm bone.
4. Stand up and lean forward. Touch the middle section of the back of your right knee with your right hand. Can you feel the tendon? What does it feel like to you?

Brain exercise
When I felt behind my knee, the tendon . . .

Activity Goal	Body Note	Key to Success	Hint
To touch two tendons and feel their connections.	Tendons move like tight cords. It is possible to see them moving under the skin. Tendons can also be seen in the neck, ankles, and other locations.	Ask a child wearing a dress or shorts to show the tendon at the back of his or her knee.	Ask children to see if they can feel the tendons in other places on their bodies.

4 Tricky Tendons—Can't Lift a Finger?

Did you know?
Your ring finger and middle finger muscles have tendons that are linked to each other.

You will need
You
Desk or table

What do you think?
If my middle finger is bent under my hand on the table, I (will) or (won't) be able to lift my ring finger.

Now you are ready to
1. Place your the fingertips of your right hand facing down on the desk.
2. Curl your middle finger underneath your hand.
3. Try to lift up your pointer finger. Can you lift it up?
4. Try to lift up your baby finger. Can you lift it up?
5. Try to lift up your ring finger. Can you lift it up?

Brain exercise
When I tried to lift up my ring finger, . . .

Activity Goal
To see how a tendon connection between fingers affects muscles.

middle
ring

Body Note
The link between the tendons on your ring finger and middle finger make them unable to move on their own. This is why the ring finger can't lift up when the middle finger is curled underneath your hand.

Key to Success
Fingertips need to be touching the table- or desktop.

Hint
You might need to help children to get their hands into the correct position.

5 Rubbery Ligaments—Secure Bones

Did you know?
Your ligaments connect bone to bone at joints.

You will need
2 wooden balls, each with one flat end (see product information, page 137)

Glue gun

1 rubber band

2 wooden cylinder shapes (find them at craft supply stores)

Your knee

What do you think?
If I connect two wooden balls on top of cylinder shapes with a rubber band, I (will) or (won't) be able to show how ligaments connect bones.

Now you are ready to
1. Use the glue gun to glue the two wooden balls to each other at their rounded sides.
2. Place the rubber band around the glued wooden balls.
3. Use the glue gun to glue a cylinder to the flat side of each wooden ball. You will be gluing the rubber band between the wooden ball and the cylinder.
4. Let the glue dry.
5. Look at what you have created. This is how your leg bones are held in place at your knee. Your ligaments are like the rubber bands holding the bones in place.

Brain exercise
Ligaments connect bone to . . .

Activity Goal	Body Note	Key to Success	Hint
To make a simple model of bone connected to bone with ligaments.	Ligaments have some elastic properties. This is why bones are sometimes dislocated. The ligaments stretch and allow the bones to move out of place.	Wooden balls need to be securely glued together so that they don't pop out of the model.	Talk to the children about how this represents bone to bone, as in a knee. Ask children to feel on the outside of their knees.

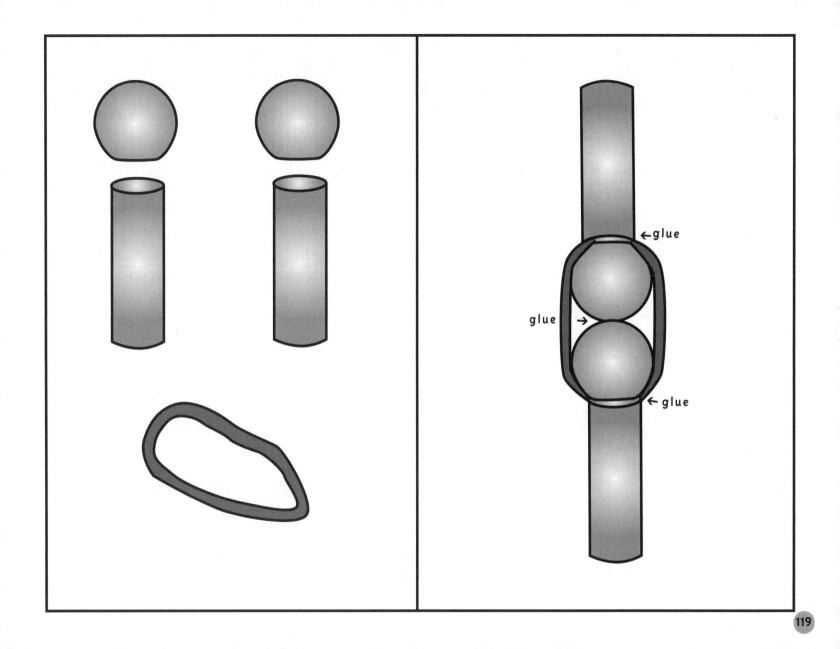

←glue

glue →

←glue

6 Bare-Bones Protection

Did you know?

Your joints are found where bones meet and move together. Bones rubbing against each other can be damaged. We call the rubbing "friction." Many bones in your body are protected from friction by the synovial fluid produced in the joints.

You will need

2 small wooden cylinders (natural, sanded finish)
2 small pieces of plastic wrap
2 short, thick rubber bands
Cooking oil

What do you think?

If I rub two wooden cylinder ends together, I (will) or (won't) be able to feel the friction between the pieces of wood.

Now you are ready to

1. Rub the wooden cylinder ends against each other. Can you feel the friction? What would happen to the cylinders if you continued to rub them together? Eventually would their surfaces be damaged?

2. Wrap the end of each block in the plastic wrap. Place the rubber bands on each block to securely hold the plastic wrap.

3. Rub the plastic-covered ends together. Do the wooden cylinders slide more easily with the plastic covering? This is similar to the effect cartilage has at the end of each bone.

4. Put a drop of oil on one of the plastic-covered wooden cylinders. Rub the cylinder ends together. The oil makes the cylinders slide easily. This is similar to how synovial fluid helps to protect and lubricate your joints from everyday wear and tear.

Brain exercise

When I rubbed the two wooden cylinder ends against each other, they . . .

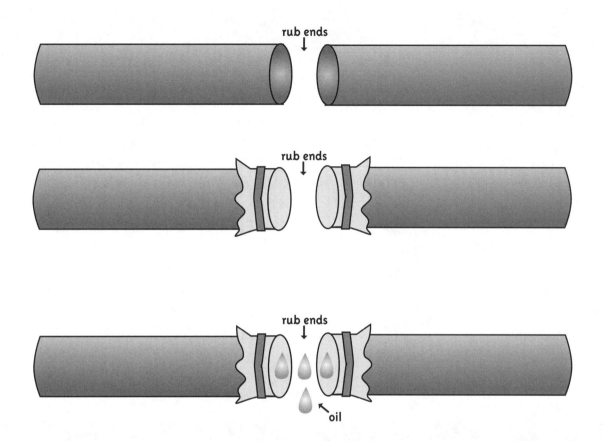

rub ends

rub ends

rub ends

oil

Activity Goal	**Body Note**	**Key to Success**	**Hint**
To demonstrate the concept of how synovial fluid protects bones.	Synovial fluid is an oil-like substance made by your body that prevents bones from damaging each other.	Make sure the cylinders have a natural sanded finish.	If wooden cylinders are unavailable, substitute two unsharpened pencils.

7 Perfect Fit—Genuine Joints

Did you know?
Each of your joints has a special position in which the bones fit together just right to support your muscles.

You will need
You
Partner

What do you think?
If I stand with my knees straight, my muscles (will) or (won't) get tired as fast as when I stand with my knees bent.

Now you are ready to
1. Stand with your knees bent while your partner counts to 30 slowly. How does this feel? Are your muscles tired? (If your muscles get too tired, stop this activity.)
2. Stand with your knees comfortably straight while your partner counts to 30 slowly. How does this feel? Was this harder or easier for your muscles?
3. Switch places with your partner. Repeat steps 1 and 2. Did your friend's muscles react the same way as yours did?

Brain exercise
When I bent my knees, my muscles . . .

Activity Goal	Body Note	Key to Success	Hint
To experience how joints help muscles save energy.	When standing upright, the knee bones fit together securely. This saves the surrounding muscles energy. They don't have to use energy to keep our bodies from collapsing.	Don't make children stand longer than is comfortable for them.	Demonstrate the knee positions before you ask children to try them.

8 It's All in Your Head—Immovable Joints?

Did you know?
The joints in your skull are fixed. This means they do not move. They are sometimes called suture joints.

You will need
Two hands
Desk

What do you think?
If the joints in my skull were movable when I was born, they (will) or (won't) be movable when I grow up.

Now you are ready to
1. Lace the fingers on both of your hands together and put them on the desk.
2. Pretend that they are stuck together and can't move anymore. That is what your skull bones are like. They have grown together and are now fixed.

Brain exercise
When I laced my fingers, they . . .

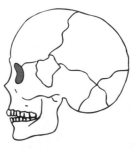

Activity Goal	Body Note	Key to Success	Hint
To visualize the concept of how joints grow together and become fixed in the skull.	By the time children reach the age of 18, all of their skull bones have grown together.	Children need to use their imaginations.	Share a big picture of the skull so children can actually see the suture lines.

9 Ball-and-Socket—Together Like a Ball and Glove

Did you know?
You have four ball-and-socket joints in your body.

You will need
Baseball
Baseball mitt

What do you think?
If I twist a baseball in a baseball mitt, I (will) or (won't) be able to show how a ball-and-socket joint works.

Now you are ready to
1. Put the baseball glove on your left hand. Form it into a cuplike shape.
2. Take the baseball with your right hand and twist the ball snugly into the mitt, going from left to right and then right to left. This is how your ball-and-socket joints work.

Brain exercise
When I twisted the ball in the mitt, it was just like . . .

Activity Goal	Body Note	Key to Success	Hint
To simulate a ball-and-socket joint. 	Ball-and-socket joints can be found in your shoulders and your hips. They allow your arms or legs to move backward and forward, up and down, and in a circle.	Do this activity and then reinforce it with activity #10, Rolling Funny Bones, page 125.	If a mitt and ball are unavailable, use a cupped hand for the mitt and a fist for the ball to demonstrate this joint. A computer joystick also works well. The children really enjoy playing with a plastic ball-and-socket building toy called Zoob Units (see product information, page 137.)

10 Rolling Funny Bones

Did you know?
Your upper arm bone is called the humerus bone. It fits into a ball-and-socket joint that allows it to roll in many different directions. This is the most flexible joint in your body.

Humerus bone →

You will need
You

What do you think?
If I wave my right arm in a circle, I (will) or (won't) be able to feel my funny bone roll at my shoulder.

Now you are ready to
1. Make a big circle with your right arm.
2. Place your left hand on your right shoulder as you make the circle.
3. Feel your right upper arm bone (humerus) roll as your right arm moves around. This is one of your four ball-and-socket joints.

Brain exercise
When I made a circle, my humerus . . .

Activity Goal	Body Note	Key to Success	Hint
To feel a ball-and-socket joint in motion.	The rounded end of the humerus fits like a ball into the socket of the shoulder bone (scapula). The ball-and-socket joint has a greater range of movement than any other type of joint.	Do activity #9, Ball-and-Socket—Together Like a Ball and Glove, page 124, before this activity to introduce the concept of ball-and-socket joints. The child needs to place his or her left hand on the shoulder joint in order to feel the movement.	Discuss the nickname "funny bone" for humerus with the children. This is very interesting to them.

Did you know?

Your hinge joints are found in your elbows, knees, jaws, and ankles.

You will need

2 shoebox lids
2 pieces masking tape
Desk

What do you think?

If I connect two shoebox lids with two pieces of masking tape, they (will) or (won't) open and close like a hinge joint.

Now you are ready to

1. Place the two shoebox lids next to each other on the desk.
2. Tape the lids together in two places (close to the top and the bottom).
3. Open and shut the lids. This is how a hinge joint works.

Brain exercise

When I opened the shoebox lids, . . .

Activity Goal	Body Note	Key to Success	Hint
To connect shoebox lids with a hingelike connection.	The hinge joint will not allow movement from side to side.	Center the masking tape between the two shoebox lids. Make sure the lids butt up to each other.	To make a more complex hinge joint, see activity #12, Build a Hinge Joint, page 127.

12 Build a Hinge Joint

Did you know?
There are more hinge joints in your body than any other type of joint.

You will need
2 wooden blocks (found at craft stores, or see product information, page 137)

Small craft hinge with 4 screws (found at craft stores, or see product information, page 137)

1 small crosspoint (Phillips) screwdriver

Table

What do you think?
If I connect two wooden blocks with a hinge joint, it (will) or (won't) open and close like a door.

Now you are ready to
1. Place the two blocks of wood next to each other on a table at the same height.
2. Center the hinge with the raised portion up on the crack between the blocks.
3. With an adult's help, use the screwdriver to screw the four small screws into the wood.
4. Open and close the blocks. The hinged blocks are similar to the hinges on a door and the hinge joint of your elbow.

Brain exercise
When I opened the blocks of wood, . . .

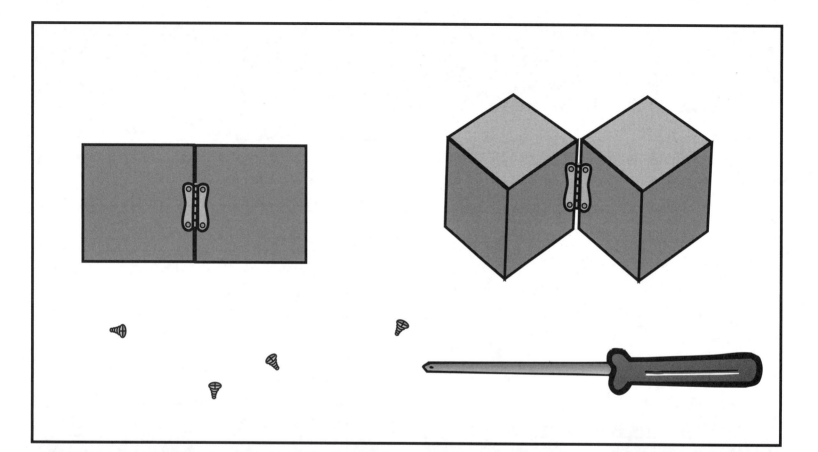

Activity Goal

To connect wood blocks with a hinge simulating the concept of a human hinge joint.

Body Note

Your hinge joints allow movement like a door opening and shutting.

Key to Success

Adult supervision is necessary when attaching the hinge to the wooden blocks. The hinge needs to lie flat on the wooden blocks.

Hint

To make a quick and simple hinge joint, see activity #11, Make a Simple Hinge Joint, on page 126.

13 Gliding Joints

Did you know?
Gliding joints are found between the bones in your toes and fingers.

You will need
2 small wooden blocks (natural, sanded finish)

What do you think?
If I slide the ends of two wooden blocks against each other in different directions, the movement (will) or (won't) be similar to the movement of my gliding joints.

Now you are ready to
1. Hold the two blocks one on top of the other.
2. Slide 1 block back and forth.
3. Slide the other block to the left and right. This is how your bones with gliding joints move together.

Brain exercise
When I slid the blocks together, it reminded me of how the bones move in my . . .

Activity Goal	Body Note	Key to Success	Hint
To simulate the concept of how a gliding joint works.	Your bones with gliding joints glide and slide next to each other to move.	Explain to the children that most bones are not flat but fit together in gliding joints like the pieces of a puzzle. They smoothly glide and slide together in a number of directions.	You could also use the wooden cylinders from activity #6, Bare-Bones Protection, page 120.

Did you know?

Your neck has a pivot joint and so does your wrist.

You will need

1 pretzel stick
1 Lifesaver

What do you think?

If I place the Lifesaver over the end of a pretzel stick, it (will) or (won't) be similar to a pivot joint.

Now you are ready to

1. Turn your head from side to side. This is called rotation.
2. Place a Lifesaver over the end of a pretzel stick. Move the Lifesaver from side to side in a half circle.

The vertebra at the top of your spine fits over a peg on the vertebra below and allows your neck and head to rotate from side to side in a way similar to the Lifesaver moving around the pretzel.

3. Turn your right wrist from side to side. You are twisting your two arm bones, the ulna and radius.
4. Move the pretzel from side to side inside the Lifesaver. This movement is similar to how your wrist bones rotate from side to side.

Brain exercise

When I moved the Lifesaver on the pretzel, it reminded me of how the bones move in my . . .

Activity Goal	Body Note	Key to Success	Hint
To explore the concept of pivot joints.	Pivot joints are only found in your wrists and spine. 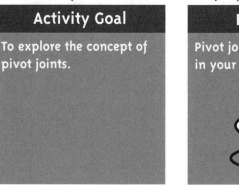	Explain to children that unlike the Lifesaver and pretzel, pivot joints allow movement from side to side rather than all the way around. This is because muscles, tendons, and ligaments limit total rotation.	Substitute a pencil or the stick of a lollipop for the pretzel. Children enjoy eating the pretzel and Lifesaver after this activity.

Did you know?

Many animals have five fingers and no thumbs. You have a very important joint found only in your thumb. It's called your saddle joint. In this joint, your bone ends are shaped like saddles and slide over each other. The saddle joint allows your thumb to tilt in all directions.

You will need

2 small Popsicle sticks
First-aid cloth tape
Adult
Your thumb
Partner
No Thumb! Data Sheet, page 132, copied onto white paper
Pencil

What do you think?

If I have a splint on my right thumb, I (will) or (won't) be able to write my name.

Now you are ready to

1. Ask an adult to make a splint for your right thumb using two Popsicle sticks and the first-aid tape. The splint should keep your thumb from bending.

2. Try writing your name with your right hand. Were you able to write? How hard was it to write? Ask your partner or an adult to mark your answers on your Data Sheet.

3. Try to eat your lunch with your right hand. Were you able to eat? How hard was it to eat? Ask your partner or an adult to mark your answers on your Data Sheet.

4. Try to pick up a book with your right hand. Were you able to pick it up? How hard was it to pick up? Ask your partner or an adult to mark your answers on your Data Sheet.

5. Try to grip a bat with your right and left hands. Were you able to grip? How hard was it to grip? Ask your partner or an adult to mark your answers on your Data Sheet.

Brain exercise

When I couldn't bend my thumb, I felt . . .

131

No Thumb! Data Sheet

Task	Yes I could	No I couldn't	How Hard? (circle) 1 2 3 easy—medium—hard
Write your name	_____	_____	1 2 3
Eat your lunch	_____	_____	1 2 3
Pick up a book	_____	_____	1 2 3
Grip a baseball bat	_____	_____	1 2 3

Watch Me Grow, © 1999. Published by Chicago Review Press, Inc., 800-888-7471.

Activity Goal	Body Note	Key to Success	Hint
To experience life without being able to use a thumb joint.	Humans and some apes have a special thumb (called an opposable thumb). It can work with each of our fingers to help us make precise movements.	A splint should go on the left thumb of a child who writes with his or her left hand.	Let all interested children try functioning without the use of the thumb joint.

16 Match Up! Where's That Joint?

Did you know?

Your joints allow you to move in many different directions.

You will need

Where's That Connection? Bingo Board, page 132, copied onto white card stock

Where's That Connection? Picture Cards, page 133, copied onto white card stock

Scissors

Answer sheet, page 136

What do you think?

If I try to match the picture cards to the Bingo Board, I (will) or (won't) match 6 out of 9 correctly.

Now you are ready to

1. Cut out all of the picture cards.
2. Look at your Where's That Connection? Bingo Board. Find the picture card you think goes with each number on the sheet.
3. Check the answer sheet, page 136, to see how many numbers you matched.
4. Did you make a bingo?
5. Try playing again later and see how much you've learned.

Brain exercise

When I first played Where's That Connection?, I . . .

Activity Goal	Body Note	Key to Success	Hint
To identify different kinds of joints in the body.	Some bones have more than one type of joint between them. The skull has many immovable joints.	Read and discuss the information in the beginning of the chapter and do the joint activities with children before they play this bingo game.	Children love learning about their joints. The bingo is a fun way for them to test their new knowledge.

Where's That Connection? Bingo Board

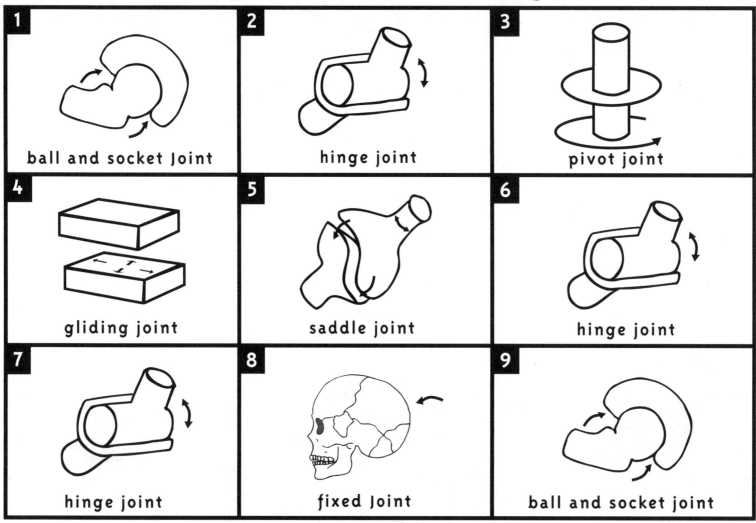

1 ball and socket Joint	**2** hinge joint	**3** pivot joint
4 gliding joint	**5** saddle joint	**6** hinge joint
7 hinge joint	**8** fixed Joint	**9** ball and socket joint

Watch Me Grow, © 1999. Published by Chicago Review Press, Inc., 800-888-7471.

Where's That Connection? Picture Cards

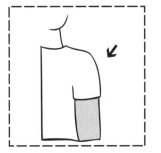

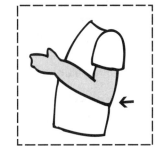

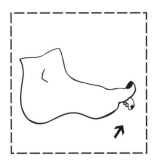

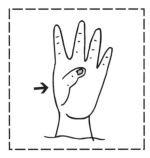

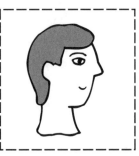

Answer Sheet

Answers to Match Up!
Where's That Bone?, *page 69*
1—Backbone (spine)
2—Hip (pelvis)
3—Shoulder, arm, and hand
4—Ear (stapes bone)
5—Head (skull)
6—Chest (rib cage)
7—Ankle and foot
8—Hand
9—Leg and foot

Answers to Bony Truths—
Name That Number!, *page 72*
1—A baby has 300+ bones at birth.
2—A hand has 27 bones.
3—An adult has approximately 206 bones.
4—An arm has 3 bones.
5—The ear has 3 bones, including the stapes, which is the smallest in the body.
6—A leg has 3 bones, including the femur (upper thigh bone), which is the largest in the body.
7—The spine has 26 bones.
8—A foot has 26 bones.
9—The face has 14 bones.

Answers to Match Up!
Where's That Joint?, *page 133*
1, 9—Hip and shoulder
2, 6, 7—Elbow, jaw, and knee
3—Neck
4—Toes
5—Thumb
8—Head

Read All About It

Author	Title	Publisher
Nick Graham	*Human Body*	Quatro Children's Books, Ltd., 1996
Trevor Day	*1001 Questions About the Human Body*	Random House, 1994
Janice VanCleave	*The Human Body*	John Wiley & Sons, Inc., 1995
Joanna Cole	*The Magic School Bus*	Scholastic Inc., 1989

Product Information

Grow, Grow, Grow
Handheld 30X microscope
Cuisenaire/Dale Seymour
1-800-237-0338
(NC088021 (Tasco) $9.50

Bundle of Bones
T Bonz (Beef Flavor)
Ralston Purina Company
St. Louis, MO 63164
$2.78

Sculpey III
Polyform Products Co.
1901 Estes Ave.
Elk Grove Village, IL 60007
#010 Translucent, $1.44

Connections
Solid wood blocks
Walnut Hollow
Rural Route 2
Dogeville, WI 53533
$1^{7}/_{8}$ in. square, no. 4104, $1.59 each

Solid wood spheres and cylinders
Provo Craft
Provo, UT 84606
$1^{1}/_{8}$ in. sphere, $ .99 each

Curved iron hinge with screws
Darice Craftwood
Strongsville, OH 44135
1.75 in. long, no. 9142-15,
2 sets, $.99

PrimOrdial Zoob Unit set
PrimOrdial
450 Geary Street, Suite 400
San Francisco, CA 94102
LLC (red/silver ball-and-socket), $6.99

Cloth measuring tape
($^{1}/_{2}$ in. wide, 5 yds long)
Johnson & Johnson
Skillman, NJ 08558-9418

Acknowledgments

Thanks to:

Debbie Braaten, physical education specialist, Christa McAuliffe Elementary School, Redmond, Washington, for her consultation and support.

Eileen Gibbons, science teacher in Rochester, New York, for her wonderful suggestions.

Deborah Hudson, arts and crafts consultant, Redmond, Washington, for her help with project materials.

Mick Malloy, QFC butcher in Redmond, Washington, for his help preparing bones for activities.

Linda Matthews, publisher, Chicago Review Press, for her thorough editing.

William Muse, biologist, Tacoma, Washington, for his recommendations.

Maureen O'Brien, nurse and homeschooling parent, Decatur, Illinois, for her insightful comments.

Gid Palmer for his sense of humor, patience, and flexibility.

Joyce Roeder, RN, school health specialist, Redmond, Washington school district, for her consultation.

Evelyn Sansky for her constant love and support.

Dr. Howard Schaengold, Redmond, Washington, for providing X rays for the children to view in A Bundle of Bones.

Stephen Yoo and Nick Palmer for their backseat editing ideas in the carpool.

Thanks to the following for their flexibility, suggestions, and opening up their classrooms to countless hours of activity testing. This book could not have been written without their support and the contributions of their eager students.

Mrs. Blakley, a first-grade teacher at Christa McAuliffe Elementary School, Redmond, Washington.

Mrs. Brown, a kindergarten teacher at Elizabeth Blackwell Elementary School, Redmond, Washington.

Mrs. Sylvestal, a second-grade teacher at Samantha Smith Elementary School, Redmond, Washington.

Thanks to Mrs. Hanson, a seventh-grade teacher at Redmond Junior High School in Redmond, Washington, for allowing me the opportunity to go through the writing process with her brilliant students as content editors. Her students helped with the reviewing, testing, and problem solving issues in the text. Their practical suggestions and problem-solving efforts contributed significantly to the writing of *Watch Me Grow*.

Student Contributors

Mrs. Brown's kindergarten class

John Castle
Anthony Delie
Kara Edwards
Nikolas Grasst
Alexis Guches
Patrick Leake
John Lee
Matthew Loh
Dylan Lovell
Chelsy Martin
Nathaniel McCammant
David Parkinson
Jeremy Rodney
Katelin Rolls
Jacob Salley
Matthew Shore
Lacy Sigman
Erin Smith
Leda Salaimani
Robert Spaulding
Clarissa Stevens
Nicola Vann

Mrs. Blakley's first-grade class

Kelsea Asher
Blake Baylor
Zachary Byrski
Michael Cofano
Garrett Daily
Alexandra Dorsey
Evan Lee
Michelle Jackson
Ian McClung
Riley Peronto
Keisha Peterson
Daniel Preston
Isabell Sakamoto
Cori Shull
Rio Simone
Emily Skubitz
Shayne Smith
Andrew Steyer
Ethan Thomas
Emily Vivian

Mrs. Sylvestal's second-grade class

Tyler Andrews
Will Baker
Raphael Bamickel
Megan Beebe
Julia Bicknell
Corbin Brokaw
Keenan Clinch
Matthew Fuget
Christopher Gordon
Chad Gray
Madeline Harig
Erik Hawes
Laura Hedeen
Stephanie Kyser
Tony Locascio
Alexa Marrs
Michael McDonald
Leona Mullen
Tyler Munno
Kallen Nelson
Magnus Olofsson
Elizabeth Orr
Duncan Sinclair
Chauncey Trask
Brent Tsujii
Alyssa Vaughan
Megan Winkel

Mrs. Hanson's seventh-grade student editors

Jesse Albert
Katie Buck
Clara Cantor
Dan Cantor
Jennifer Cushing
Joscelyn Doleac
Brock Erwin
Anna Eschenburg
Tammy Guo
Jesse Heilman
Andrew Hopps
Jillian Houck
Emily Hu
David Lee
Emmett Nicholas
Rob Ohlstrom
Stephanie Orrico
Tyler Sargent
Peter Simonson
Debbie Weiser
Jammie Wu

More exciting science activity books from Chicago Review Press

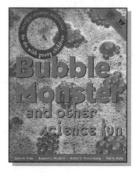

Bite-Sized Science
Activities for Children in 15 Minutes or Less
John H. Falk and Kristi S. Rosenberg
Quick, innovative activities to get young minds discovering the wonders of the natural world by making predictions, testing them, and then evaluating the results.

ages 3–8
ISBN 1-55652-348-3
144 pages, paper, $12.95

Bubble Monster
And Other Science Fun
John Falk, Robert L. Pruitt II, Kristi S. Rosenberg, and Tali A. Katz
Forty-five fun science activities created by the ScienceMinders project of the YWCA of Annapolis and Anne Arundel County.

"Easy-to-follow directions. . . . A useful purchase."
—*School Library Journal*
"I recommend this book for every parent."
—*New York Hall of Science*

ages 3–8
ISBN 1-55652-301-7
176 pages, paper, $17.95

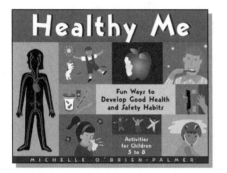

Healthy Me
Fun Ways to Develop Good Health and Safety Habits
Michelle O'Brien-Palmer

More than 70 creative projects, recipes, and experiments that promote health and safety.

ages 4—8
ISBN 1-55652-359-9
160 pages, paper, $12.95

Sense-Abilities
Fun Ways to Explore the Senses
Michelle O'Brien-Palmer

Dozens of fun and original science activities that explore taste, touch, sight, smell, and hearing.

"These great ideas should be welcomed by teachers."
—*School Library Journal*

ages 4—8
ISBN 1-55652-327-0
176 pages, paper, $12.95